SEVEN LIVES:

A Diva's Story

D0731810

BY DIANE MORRISON

Table of Contents

Prologue

My mother, Veronica, wrote in my baby book on November 24, 1946, my fourth birthday:

I watched you grimace this morning as you took all twenty-five of your pink curlers out. You wanted banana curls, even though you knew it would be hard to sleep on so many curlers. I put a tiny bit of soft pink rouge on your plump cheeks and a little more on your lips. Grandma Addie laughed when you did a little Irish jig in her honor.

"You look like a sweet Colleen," Addie said.

"What is a Colleen?" you asked.

"You know, it's all about your fiery red hair and your fiery ways," Addie told you in her best Irish brogue.

The photographer's studio had mini rooms: one room had a cozy red chair and a bookshelf of picture books, one room had a hardback oak chair with a small desk full of little dolls dressed in costumes from other countries. Your favorite room was painted white with lace curtains on the windows and a big bench.

You chose the white room, which surprised me. Before the photographer began, you said your legs were cold in the short pink and blue skirt you picked out. The photographer moved the heavy mahogany bench by a sunny window for you. He promised you could cover your legs when he was done taking pictures.

You turned into a young Diva as you sat upright in your dressiest clothes, no longer Cookie, a nickname your father gave you. I watched you shift your eyes toward Pop, looking for his approval. He smiled at you, then you put on a performance.

Over the years, I discover being a Diva is not limited to being a show off, self-important, pretentious, or even obnoxious. I'm certainly not an "opera singer," part of the definition of the word *diva* in Webster's dictionary. I define a Diva, male or female, as a person who is strong, self-aware, and free of society's boxes.

I am an awakening Diva. I will never exile any part of myself. Acceptance is what awakening is, in the truest sense. It's about loving my decadent side, loving my crappy side, loving my beautiful side, loving my messy side, loving the connoisseur, loving the Diva. It's about seeing the whole image of myself—a combination of my seven styles of Diva defined by my seven nicknames: Rare Orchid: a survivor, Tough Cookie: a performer, Ginger: an academy girl, Princess: a wife, Gypsy: a free-spirited single woman, Diva: a wealthy entrepreneur, Collector: an art connoisseur.

1

The Psychic

Like a lot of women, the seminal moment in my life is the day I find out I have breast cancer and having my right breast cut off on March 17, 1981, Saint Patrick's Day. The days after my surgery are full of questions. *Will I die? Will my marriage survive? Will my friends and family treat me differently? How will I deal with my mangled chest?*

During the months and years after surviving breast cancer, I seek mentors who help me tell a story about how I stepped into my true Diva-ness that we see in full-bloom during and after my divorce on May 5, 1994. The truth is that I was an unconscious Diva until cancer woke me up. From then on, I chose to be conscious and free.

My story begins in a psychic's office in Boulder, Colorado, on September 10, 1993. I'm expecting to meet a gypsy with wild, red, curly hair, but Dora, as she calls herself, has slick black hair, pulled back away from her face in a long ponytail. Her deep black eyes are piercing and seem to be seeing into my soul. I imagine she may have started doing her work as a palm reader in a tent somewhere in a mountain town in Colorado, but clearly Dora is moving up in the metaphysical world with her rather posh office in downtown Boulder.

Her assistant, Tom, is in charge of all the business details and he follows her around like a trained pup. Maybe the only things remaining from her previous set-up are the clattering beaded curtains I have to walk through to enter her reading room, a crystal ball, and at least ten lit candles sitting on an Asian dressing table. There's also something on the wall that looks like a family heirloom, perhaps a coat of arms. Clearly Dora is eccentric with eclectic taste. *Is this whole thing a farce?* I ask myself. Her male secretary moves from his black lacquered desk to set up a silver tea service for us. He leads me to a purple velvet loveseat, stacked with burgundy velvet pillows that have hand-stitched *RL* in gold letters—these pillows were purchased at Ralph Lauren. Oddly, the rug under the loveseat is white, which isn't in line with the rest of the decor.

As I sip my tea cautiously, not wanting to spill even a drop on the rug, I take a second look around the room, wondering why there are cheesy beads from the seventies hanging between Dora's office and this room. Does she want to hold onto a gypsy personality, yet give her client, me, a hint she's making enough money to own designer furniture?

I want to buy into what Dora is going to say about me, but I keep asking myself if she's authentic. Are any of us really authentic? While I wait, I shake the beaded curtain for the sound effect and I run my hands over the pillows for tactile pleasure as I slip on Dora's long, multi-colored silk robe, hoping she doesn't have a hidden camera. I continue to wonder if my decision to come here with questions about whether or not to get a divorce was ill-considered. Should I have read more reviews about Dora beforehand? In spite of all my suspicions that this experience is a scam, I consider some of the weirdness about her adds a spiritual vibe to the room. It could be the smell of so many candles burning. Is this real or am I in a dream?

"Charmed to meet you, Diane," Dora says as she gives me a strong, almost parental, hug.

Her perfume is pungent. Later she tells me she's wearing Black Orchid from Paris. I compliment her on her white business suit and white Prada heels, but the multi-colored chandelier earrings are a telltale sign of her former gypsy life. Nonetheless, I conclude I'm getting advice from a business woman who has a strong personality type, perhaps a black and white instinctual type—tough, with a big heart. I start to anticipate her advice will be clear and concise without innuendo.

"How are you, Diane?" Dora asks as she holds out both hands as if she's welcoming me to her private den. "Thanks for sending your time of birth. Seeing your astrology chart gives me a framework of your life."

Next she opens a jewel box full of what looks like pieces that would be used in a board game. She lays out two for me. "These objects are symbols of the key aspects of your astrology chart. Choose one at a time," she says, as if I know what the hell she's talking about.

"The arrow stands for your sun sign, Sagittarius. You're fiery, eccentric, and adventurous. You can pick up the twins now because your moon is in Gemini. The combination of these signs prove you are clever and very lucky. You are optimistic and funny people will always want to be around you. Have you thought about being an entrepreneur? The public school system must be restrictive for you. Perhaps you could choose writing or speaking, or both, as new careers. You're a risk-taker. You can go for a new career now. It's time for a change."

Her almost purple lips spread to form a slightly imperceptible sign of acknowledgement of who she thinks I am. Dora begins chanting in a deep, guttural voice as she invites a variety of deities into the room: Mother Mary, Quan Yin, and Shakti. It is Boulder; goddesses are in style here! I keep my eyes closed, partly out of respect for Dora's performance and partly because

I'm freaking out. The chanting stops, but Dora suggests I keep my eyes closed.

After we move on to her meeting room, Dora says, "You mentioned in your intake email you have been called a *Diva* most of your life. Tell me how that started, and feel free to share any memories of being a performer, which you also mentioned in your correspondence."

"Well," I say, "my baby book has a telegram glued inside: Dear Daddy, you have a beautiful, eight-pound girl. Mother and baby are doing fine, signed Pops. In my opinion, it could have said: Dear Daddy, you're the proud father of a baby Diva."

Dora looks away for a minute to avoid laughing as I read from my stained, slightly tattered, baby book.

"The day I was born was a cold day. I popped out of the womb a month early on November 24. I entered this world on my own terms. The doctor who delivered me called me a rare orchid because my chances of survival at that time were a million to one. My twin brother exited at four months. Maybe he sensed the miserable life that was coming for him. My father, Robert, wanted to name me Ginger because I had red streaks in my hair. My mother, Veronica, had the last word. She named me Diane, which is entered in my baby book, to let everyone know I am meant to be a Diva, a goddess. Veronica dreamed we would live in a beautiful brownstone in Brooklyn and she would dress me in clothes from Saks Fifth Avenue. Life would be divine!"

"What is being a Diva like for you, Diane?" Dora asks.

"Well, I need my beauty sleep. I make grand entrances. I'm a prima donna, snapping my fingers wherever I go. My clothes are designer brands. You might call me entitled."

"You could think of being a Diva as a protection. It probably saved you as a child, but as an adult, it might make you a target for harsh remarks and even jealousy. Remember this, Diane: it's never too late to have a happy childhood. Do you mind if I tape my predictions for your future now? You'll get a copy of the tape, of course."

Dora takes a few minutes to ponder my left hand because it is close to my heart. She doesn't say anything about my hand, not even a mention of my life line. I remind myself the astrology piece was accurate. Is she a phony or is she real? This is an act, but a good one. I open myself to the drama. On her request, we hold hands for a minute, using a simple humming mantra. Then she proceeds with her predictions, just as the friend who recommended her said she would. Since this friend lives in Boulder, he checks in with Dora now and then and calls her his therapist. I guess he thinks I'm starting to look like a train wreck. Well, one thing is clear, I'm in the middle of kind of a psychodrama.

"Diane, you are more than a new identity: you are a new incarnation in the same body. Divorce is the best thing for you at this point in your life. When we spoke on the phone, you called yourself a strong, self-assured woman. You also mentioned you experienced a difficult childhood, followed by a marriage to a controlling husband who always referred to you as *Princess* until you developed breast cancer. I see the whole Diva transition, both in your palm and in your astrology chart. Many experts believe the concept of the Diva is actually a triad. You started as a Damsel-in-Distress until age eleven, followed by a Princess, and now, as you approach divorce, you are truly embracing Diva, flavored with traces of a perpetual adolescent."

Now this is a bit much. I'm not into this new incarnation stuff. It sounds like a bunch of New Age mumbo jumbo. "And the Oscar goes to Dora," I'm tempted to blurt out!

Tom sticks his head through the beaded curtain. "There are two fire trucks lined up outside the Boulder Theater. Please excuse us, Miss Diane. There might be a fire in one of Boulder's landmark buildings," he says.

"Can we reconvene after lunch? A very good friend of mine purchased the theater recently. It has been closed for a year. He's out of the state right now. I'm in charge of the comings and goings connected with the theater," Dora quickly grabs her coat and leaves.

"Of course! I will get some lunch and return in an hour?" I say to Tom.

I order a shake at an ice cream store on the Pearl Street Mall, then move on to the antique store next door. The owner is obviously a fan of music from the thirties because he's playing "Animal Crackers in My Soup." I can't help singing along with Shirley Temple. Of course, I purchase the record and some old magazines with young Shirley on the cover.

I've a feeling that when Dora returns she's going to ask me more about my childhood. I look at my watch. I have another half-hour to let memories surface before Dora returns to her office.

It was a cold snowy night the first time my Uncle Frank asked me to perform. He helped me with my winter coat so that we could go outside to make a snow girl. My mother smoked Lucky Strikes in our bedroom while listening to *The Shadow* on the radio. Frank and I ran out before she noticed. While my uncle and I played in the snow, he teased me about pretending to be Shirley Temple.

"Cookie, could you do a little dance in the snow like Shirley Temple did in *The Bachelor* and *The Bobby Soxer*, the movie we saw last month at Aunt Gracie's movie theater? Didn't Veronica buy you a bunch of her records?"

I was five, growing up in Jersey City, when I began performing for my family, but I didn't start with a Shirley Temple dance.

"Come on, Cookie, give us a song, how about a little dance? Or you could read one of your stories? You always put a smile on my face," Frank pleaded earlier that year. Frank came to dinner every Sunday night. We said grace, ate dinner, and then he expected me to perform. The plan was for me to be a distraction when the heavy drinking started, what Frank called "getting sozzled." Frank loved me to perform. He was one of the few people in the family who saw me as a star instead of the poor, fatherless child of a war hero. He treated me like a normal kid. I usually started Sunday nights with a tap dance, wearing my black patent-leather shoes with pink satin ribbon ties. Sometimes I'd follow the dance by reciting "Fuzzy Wuzzy Was a Bear" while I held a teddy bear and wore my Fuzzy Wuzzy robe.

Fuzzy Wuzzy was a bear
Fuzzy Wuzzy had no hair
Fuzzy Wuzzy was not fuzzy
Was he?
Fuzzy Wuzzy lost his hair
In a North Pole Barber chair
Fuzzy Wuzzy was not fuzzy
Was he?

Fuzzy Wuzzy always got a round of applause and more coins on the table for my piggy bank. I got another round of applause when Frank helped me tell a story about British troops learning to respect Arabic troops who were with them on the battlefield. These troops were called "Fuzzy Wuzzy" because of their hair.

I typically extended my hands, curling my fingers toward me, which signaled to my audience that I wanted more coins for my short history lesson. I was a Diva like Shirley Temple, who started performing at a young age. I started wearing curly hair because I wanted to look like her. I could do all of her hand movements the way she did when she tap danced.

Aunt Gracie helped dress me for special dinners. It's time for me to pick something special from what she calls her "magic shopping bag" tonight. She usually offers me tiny purses, embroidered hankies, costume jewelry, and white gloves. Gracie was fun, especially when she visited for New Year's Eve.

"Just a minute, I'll be right back, Cookie. You can pick four more things tonight," she giggled.

I played dress-up with Gracie's clothes, choosing a beaded black purse, a velvet hat called a *pill box*, a pair of white gloves that button over a single white pearl, and a pair of silver high heels.

When Gracie returned to the room, she helped me get ready to become Shirley Temple for my next performance. When we're done, she takes pictures of me. I posed like I was going to be on the cover of a magazine. "Aren't you the little Diva," Gracie said, as she tucked dollar bills into my Shirley Temple purse. I whispered in her ear I wanted to be someone famous.

Before I went out of the room, Gracie gave me a small holy picture of Saint Teresa, my favorite saint, to put under the bottom sheet on my bed. "It's a protection," Gracie said, as if she knew something about why I needed protection in my bed.

I forgot about what Gracie said when I entered the dining room in a red dress with white polka dots wearing my shiny Shirley Temple flats as I held my purse with Shirley's name on the front. Finally, Gracie put a rhinestone crown on top of my curly, red hair. I am Shirley Temple!

My mother, Veronica, looked beautiful on that New Year's Eve, the last night of 1947. Her high heels matched her red silk dress. Her makeup was perfect. It was as if she expected to become a new person, perhaps start a new life, the next day. I wondered if she would have a date with someone next year. She looked so lonely. Veronica sat at the table like a Diva herself, while Gracie did all the work of getting me ready for my performances. Gracie was a helper. She never married because she took care of her mother until the day Nora died at ninety-five.

The Christmas lights are still turned on late that night. Gracie does some cleaning up before she gets me out of my Shirley Temple clothes. Gracie's house always looks clean and smells like rose petals. I can't wait to visit there tomorrow on New Year's Day. Plates of sugar cookies will be waiting for me. I take the ones shaped like bells because I like the sound of bells.

Gracie and I listened to my mother's problems, her unending sad story about losing my father. "Poor thing, you have a hard life, Veronica. Jesus, Mary, and Joseph, you need to get out of that house. Too much drinking there," Gracie's mother, Nora, told my mother.

I was a resilient child. I would tell myself, *It's okay. I will be okay. My family loves me.* I never saw myself as a victim. I see now I was polishing my Diva skills of manipulating and getting my way at a young age.

I arrive back at Dora's office before she returns. The office lights are dim . . . or does it just feel that way because Dora isn't there? Tom seems different when she's gone. It's *her* energy that fills the place. Tom talks with me about his boss, who he is clearly in love with.

"Dora studied psychology, but she prefers to read palms and make predictions, which is unusual. She was born in central Italy, close to Turin, I think," he says with pride.

I knew Dora was a gypsy putting on a good show!

"You look so familiar to me, Tom. Did you ever take one of my graduate courses?" I ask.

"You have quite a memory, Diane. Yes, I was dating a teacher in Denver about five years ago. My girlfriend and I took one of your Enneagram classes. I took the class for non-credit. You are such a memorable professor, with your wild red hair and those Prada sunglasses. It really is a small world," he says, with a hearty chuckle.

Since Dora is still detained at the Boulder Theater, Tom sets up another appointment for the following week. He mentions Dora would like me to join her in her home in Boulder Canyon for the next meeting.

When Dora and I come back together in her home, which is less eccentric than her office style, I conclude my psychic is a very creative person. She added unicorns, fairies, butterflies, and other fanciful creatures with strokes of various shades of blue paint on the otherwise stark white walls in her living room. There are large pieces of colorful glass on contemporary side tables throughout the room. Unlike the soft velvet furniture in her office, the furniture here is in white leather topped with colorful pillows and soft cashmere throws to add warmth to the leather. There are certain features in Dora's home that remind me of the home my husband and I are building in Roxborough Park, which is close to where I teach in south Denver. I wonder if my dream home will end up being sold in a divorce settlement. I would try to keep it, but I'm sure Anthony will not allow that, even though I've spent a year designing it.

"Tom tells me you teach classes on the Enneagram. What is your personality type?" Dora asks.

"I'm a Type 7, the adventurous risk-taker. Which lines up with what you told me about my astrology chart, right?"

Dora agrees with my assessment of who I appear to be, noting that the Enneagram is primarily about my ego. After she hands me a tall glass of Champagne, she focuses on how I have been protected by my father all of my life. She claims Robert has stayed close to me from the spiritual realm. "He watched all of your performances when you were a child, and he watches them now," she says, as if she can see him sitting on one of her leather couches now.

"Yes, well, I've thought of Robert as an angel floating above my head, never real to me. Since his medals and commendation were visible to me, it was not as if I could escape the fact my father died saving another soldier's life."

Who is this woman? Whoever she is, I will be seeing her often as I prepare to get a divorce.

Dora asks me if I liked performing as a child. She wonders if I felt performing in front of a bunch of drunks was abusive.

"To tell you the truth, I was born to perform," I say, as if what I did was perfectly normal. "I really thought I was another Shirley Temple. I loved the attention."

"Tell me more about how you became a performer at such a young age," Dora requests.

I stand up in the middle of Dora's living room, putting on a performance of "Alphabet Soup," almost like I did when I was five years old, although a kitchen chair was my first stage back then.

"I hear my Uncle Frank yell out, 'your Majesty' as he took a bow to honor me when I entered the room. The coins hit the table before I even started performing because everyone loves Shirley Temple. I scooped up the coins into my purse as fast as I could. I know now I only have to look like a Diva to make money. While I performed, out came the usual brown bottles of beer and sometimes a bottle of Irish whiskey, along with my grandmother Addie's collection of shot glasses, which she claimed were passed down from the McDonald clan, her father's side of the family. When Addie got into her shots, she would require that I do an Irish Jig with her. I wonder if my uncles and Pop could see my panties when I kicked up my legs. I'm guessing they did, because I got three times more coins than usual for an Irish jig. There was excessive drinking and singing, mostly Irish songs."

I see tears falling from Dora's dark eyes as she holds me until I come back to the present moment. "What your family did to you was abusive, but because of your positive personality traits you didn't see it that way. You saw it as a way to be free, a way to get out of Jersey City, because you saved the money you earned performing for your family. It's all about perception, Diane."

Now Dora is laughing a short, spiky laugh as if she can identify with what I'm saying because she too is a performer.

Her final words to me that evening are, "Diane, you are going to be wealthy. Agents will be knocking on your door. There's a published book in your future. You need help with technology before you create the book. Take a class. You are going to be a true Diva, owning your own company, becoming a successful, wealthy woman. Be sure you continue to seek your true self as you are on an amazing new journey. I hope to see you again soon."

As I leave the psychic for the second time, I still feel my experiences with her were a performance more than anything else. I understand performance, because I use it all the time. I love it when I'm acting like a pretentious Diva. My Uncle Frank believed I could be anything I wanted to be. He would say things like, "Someday you'll be Miss America or a famous actress, Cookie."

2

Last Dance

Before I leave Boulder after an intense session with Dora, I walk to Pearl Street for happy hour. It's a warm breezy evening at a small outdoor cafe with a nice view of the Flatirons. The waitress offers me a menu, mentioning wines and wells are half-price and appetizers are a dollar off. I narrow the people-watching down to three tables: a group of women who are wearing exercise clothes, a student wearing a Naropa University shirt, and an older and attractive man who looks like he could be a professor because he is grading papers he took out of his leather briefcase. Apparently, the young women teach yoga in a small studio close to the cafe. As I listen to their conversations about men and how they love being single, I wonder what my life would have been like if I hadn't married at twenty. Would I have chosen to be a therapist as I had planned, remaining single until I had established a successful practice, perhaps on the west coast? What if I had applied to UCLA Berkeley, got a scholarship, and never met Anthony? I knew I was smart—the only girl for generations to get into college. Quite an accomplishment in the late fifties. Resisting the urge to have conversations with the people around me, I start sipping my Grey Goose vodka and tonic, finally taking a quick look at the written assignment Dora gave me before I left the canyon.

Dora wrote: I sense you are repressing your true feelings about having breast cancer and your husband's reaction to your body after the mastectomy. Any woman who doesn't give a damn about losing a breast is abandoning a part of herself. It's time for you to feel the anger about your loss or you will burn up. Call me after you write down old memories of that recovery time in your life. Remember you are starting a new life, which means letting go of the past. Don't hold back in your writing. I put Dora's note aside because the older man is approaching me.

"You look like you are in deep thought tonight, miss. Buy you another drink?"

After I tell him I'm headed back to Denver in a few minutes, he insists on picking up my tab as he hands me a business card.

"You never know when you might need your pipes cleaned out," he laughs.

I tuck his card in my blouse, thinking that although I was wrong about him being a professor, he's charming and playful in a provocative way.

When I return to our temporary apartment, I put Dora's note on my desk, kick off my heels, and throw down my purse. As soon as I lay across the ugly gold couch in our temporary home, Anthony pokes his head in the door. I wonder if he overheard me talking to a friend about Dora just before I started to doze off.

He starts pacing the floor, "I want to go back to the way things were with us in the sixties. I thought the sex was great then. You will always be my fraternity dream girl because you got along so well with my fraternity brothers. I'll never forget your costumes for our toga parties. You could make yourself look like a pin-up girl," Anthony says.

"Come on, Anthony, you're just worried I will divorce you. I know how the Catholic church views divorce."

"You know I will be excommunicated from the church. What will my parents think?"

Of course I don't agree with what Anthony is saying. My Diva nature, which has been somewhat restricted in our marriage, causes me to push the envelope around the church's attitude about divorce, which he brings up daily as he senses I'm pulling away from him. The church doesn't condone divorce, threatening excommunication. Remarriage is considered adultery, and there's still a hint one could be condemned to hell as the result of getting a divorce. Clearly, Anthony believes all of those archaic decrees of the church.

I have always struggled with the church's teachings about relationships, particularly anything concerning sex. Sex is only for procreation, which of course doesn't work because birth control is still forbidden in the early nineties. As if sweating about getting pregnant isn't enough, masturbation is considered a sin. I'm too full of hormones to only think about my husband's sexual fulfilment. Honestly, I wonder if any Catholic woman feels authentic in the nineties.

"Remember the low-cut, tight, emerald green wool dress I bought at Saks Fifth Avenue earlier in the day before New Year's Eve in 1964, Anthony? You insisted the dress would be perfect with black leather pumps, black net stockings, and that beaded purse you gave me for Christmas. After dinner that night we went to a hotel with a ballroom; I can't remember the name of the hotel, but we danced and danced until people gathered around us. They were clapping as you spun me into dizziness."

"Yes, you were beautiful that night, but I have always thought you were the most beautiful the night we first met at a dance at Newman Hall before classes started at WVU."

I want to mention to him that he was pompous the night we met, introducing himself by showing his Mensa card with his high IQ—145, as I recall. And what about the fact that he literally stalked me from then on? Anthony stood outside the door of every one of my classes as if it was a random circumstance. He later admitted he spent hours predicting which classes I would most likely attend. But I didn't mention any of my annoyance about his stalking, not even the night he tried to pin me before I was really ready for a marriage proposal.

I remember standing on the balcony of my dorm, wearing my black, chiffon cocktail dress with expensive, strappy gold shoes as Anthony's fraternity brothers sang to me. I had several photographs of that night. The fraternity brothers were dressed in black tuxedos. Anthony attached his fraternity pin to a bow that was tied on a bouquet of a dozen red roses. He blushed when I wouldn't allow him to place the pin on my dress.

When I went back to my room, I replaced my cocktail dress with a silk toga nightgown designed by my Aunt Iris, a famous lingerie designer. Apparently Iris married my uncle William for his English surname. They both agreed his name would get her through the war years since she was a Jew designing lingerie for American and European markets.

I can imagine Iris adjusting her long string of Chanel pearls when William handed her a small bouquet of pink sweetheart roses the day they married. I wonder if Iris ever regretted marrying a gay man.

I didn't sleep the night I refused Anthony's pin. When I finished my last Marlboro, I wrote down the names of all the bad boys I had dated. Anthony was never a bad boy; he was predictable, intelligent, and I expected he would be successful.

Anthony gave me what I needed: two beautiful children and a typical suburban life from the sixties through the eighties. He treated me like a princess, pampering me in a possessive sort of way. I never felt real with him. I was more like his show-horse. Anthony loved to see other men hit on me at social events. It was like this until I got breast cancer in the eighties.

After the cancer, he shut me down. I was no longer perfect for the ultimate perfectionist. When I truly realized this, along with the fact he never touched my right breast again, not even after I got implants, I filed separation papers. It was two weeks before our thirtieth anniversary. The only sadness I felt was I would never live in the house Anthony and I were building on a property south of Denver between a state park and a national park. I did most of the design work for the project, buying unusual pieces, such as hand-painted sinks and white-washed doors, both from Santa Fe, New Mexico. There was even an artist's studio in the back of the house with large windows, heavy oak floors, and a big sink that looked more like a wash tub.

The day before I file for a separation, he asks me to meet him at our favorite Italian restaurant. I feel my mind wandering as Anthony refuses to give me eye contact while he quickly downs two beers.

"Where is your wedding ring?" Anthony screams, alerting everyone in the restaurant.

"I'll take another Chianti, please," I tell our waitress, who looks concerned for me. She and I had met earlier when I started drinking before Anthony arrived. I take another sip of Chianti, noticing the deep redness of the wine on my lips, which actually looks like lipstick on my open mouth. I use the mirror next to us to look at Anthony's reflection. His critical nature keeps him from accepting that my not wearing my wedding ring was a simple mistake on my part. I must have left it on the sink that morning before washing my hands. I was late for a staff meeting.

Rather than answering him, I just watch his anger surface like fire. Fire burns. Fire leaves marks. I make a point of remembering that, although I don't remember much of what he said that night, just that he was loud.

After Anthony laid down a fifty-dollar bill and stormed out of the restaurant, people actually clapped, thinking, I assume, they would finally be able to eat their meals in peace.

"This one is on the house. What a jerk!" my waitress says as she sets down one more Chianti.

Exactly three weeks later, Anthony moves to a cheaper apartment. I remain in the apartment where I've been living for the last year.

It's a cold windy night in mid-September, the kind of night you might share hot chocolate or a hot toddy by a warm fire with a close friend or lover. Anthony is neither. I meet him on his own grounds as he's requested a meeting to discuss our marriage.

He doesn't greet me or offer to take my coat when I enter his apartment. Just as well because it's freezing. The kitchen is stark with nothing on the white walls, lacking color or warmth, like a prison cell. Water drips into the pitted white sink, matching the same rhythm as the small brass clock Anthony has had since childhood. The sounds give me a sense of rhythm, which calms me. As if the lack of heat in the room isn't enough to send a chill through my body, Anthony sits a glass of ice water in front of me. I think about the last ten or so years of this aloof, unloving relationship I have tolerated with the man in front of me. The man I married, who crosses T's before he writes them. Always a perfectionist. But my body isn't perfect to him anymore. He can't look me in the eyes as he pulls something that looks like a grocery list out of his shirt pocket.

"I'm angry you had breast surgery! Did you even think about how that would affect our sex life?" he asks.

"So what did you want me to do Anthony, die?"

Years later, life offers a convergence of coincidences. Some might call what happened to Anthony *karma*. Not that I would ever wish my ex-husband anything bad, but he did end up with prostate cancer, which I'm sure affected his sex life with his second wife.

"You have not been performing your wifely duties to my satisfaction, Diane. Call me when you're ready to be a proper wife again," he says as he walks out of the room, leaving me sitting on a cold, metal bar stool with a cold glass of water.

Rather than go after him with something like, "You selfish son of a bitch!" I focus on what I have to do tomorrow to end my marriage to one of the coldest, most unfeeling men I have ever met.

I feel knackered the next morning because I had several shots of tequila before I slipped under a pile of blankets. When I call my lawyer, he sets up an appointment for me to sign formal divorce papers. My lawyer, in contrast to the man I have been married to for thirty years, is a real mensch, coming from a place of integrity. Does the black yarmulke on his skull this afternoon signal he is an orthodox Jew? The Pope wears a white skull cap. Someday I will find out what these caps mean.

After Larry and I have pastrami sandwiches, lunch turns into a friendly meeting with a skilled coach who happens to be my lawyer. He suggests that I spend the rest of the day at the bank emptying my security box, taking Anthony's name off my accounts, and by evening, writing a simple will.

Anthony is served with papers at work that afternoon. He calls me the next day to let me know he's moving out of his apartment to live with a friend he met at a church dance recently. It's hard for me to keep from laughing when he asks that he not be served anything else at his office, stating he has a reputation to maintain. "Reputation," I want to say, "you have had the same unimpressive job your whole career," but I don't.

There's something about the finality of filing for divorce that gives me the woolies, as my grandmother Addie would say. I get into a cycle of contemplating *what if* scenarios, especially at night, remembering Anthony's obsession with me. It's not that my marriage was ever physically volatile, but his significant collection of guns remain stored in my apartment. I tell Larry about how Anthony used to say if I ever divorced him, it would be divorce Italian style—his way of saying he would shoot me.

"Anthony doesn't want any other man to have you, Diane. I suggest you change all of your locks and get a storage unit for the guns. If necessary, I will get a restraining order. Let me know if you need to talk to a therapist. I will make sure Anthony pays the fees as part of the divorce settlement," Larry says.

"I'm seeing a psychic and getting massage therapy to deal with the divorce," I tell him.

When Larry asks me why I stayed in an unhealthy marriage for so long, I realize the Catholic Church gave me reason to feel guilty about getting a divorce, and I wanted to raise my children in what I thought was a traditional family.

"Your true personality must have been repressed during your marriage, Diane, but you seem ready to take on the power of a strong Diva, as you refer to yourself often," he says.

"Any woman can be a Diva, Larry. I'm feeling more and more like a savvy go-getter coming into my prime as a fifty-three-year-old, soon to be single, woman who is ready to become an entrepreneur as soon as the dust settles after my divorce." I hear lightning bolts that sound like demons being released on the street; the universe is letting me know I have the strength to finalize my divorce tomorrow.

Anthony's face is beet red as he signs the divorce papers on May 5, 1994. He waves his fist at my lawyer and me as he storms out of the office.

Larry and I share a glass of Champagne as we watch the sunset from his large window overlooking the city. "Diane, I didn't tell you my mother died of breast cancer. You're wise to leave a toxic relationship. I admire your strength. Pay attention to your psychic. Write that memoir someday. I can't wait to read it. Maybe I'll see you in the Park soon. The Park would be a perfect place for you to live, by the way."

3

City Life

It's early July when I start looking at properties close to downtown Denver. I have missed out on getting contracts on five homes and two condos, which makes me think it would make more sense to live in a condo close to my school, south of Denver. My lawyer's suggestion about living in his neighborhood comes to mind one sunny Saturday afternoon when I end up at the Park neighborhood to have a picnic with a friend.

After my fourth week searching the area with my realtor, we are just about to call it a day when we stumble upon a 1900s bungalow just two blocks from the park. The earthy stone exterior of the house reminds me of the house I designed and lost in the divorce settlement. When I get inside the property, it's a combination of a southwest and French design. The large titanium windows become a focal point in the living room. The brochure points out the fact that the red and white oak floors date back to 1900. The eleven-foot ceilings give a sense of airiness that is unusual for most bungalows.

There's only one problem: the mortgage is half my salary. I walk around the park for hours after my realtor leaves. My mind drifts back to the ways I earned money performing for my family as a child. The entrepreneur in me nudges me hard. I take a leap of faith. I will find another way to earn money besides teaching in the public schools. I make an offer from a small cafe within walking distance of what I believe to be my next home.

An old friend approaches me as I'm sipping my coffee. The minute I see Julian, I remember a letter I wrote to him a few years ago but never sent. If I could love you the way I want to Julian, how would I love you? We would be together every day: walking, talking, laughing, traveling. I have known you all my life, even before I knew my own name. Your breath has always been with me. Your smile lights me up. You are my love.

"My God, Diane, how are you. You look more beautiful than ever. What are you doing in this area?"

"Would you excuse me for a minute, Julian, I need to make an urgent phone call?" I ask.

When I return to my table, Julian is gone, but he's left a note with his current phone number and a single line: *Come back to me!*

A month later, I'm living in my dream house. After I settle in, I realize I bought a very impractical but beautiful home. Three major things are missing: closets, kitchen cabinets, and a dishwasher. I don't care because I love the place. It will evolve with me as I evolve. Since I'm just ten minutes from the city of Denver, I feel as if I'm back in New York in the fifties. Like my neighborhood in New York, I can walk to a bakery, a meat store, and an ice cream store like I did in my teens. What else could I possibly want? Mornings are either for walking around the different lakes in the park, just two blocks away, or writing in cafes or coffee shops, also within walking distance. The area is perfect for me. Clearly being here is opening my mind to some lofty goals. I visualize a life of possibilities. I'm free!

As I continue to sip my coffee at Dottie's Café, I wonder why beautiful, amazing Divas like me stay in loveless marriages. Many stay for the kids. I did that, even though my son and daughter were not small children. I wanted the facade of a traditional family, whatever the hell that was in the nineties. I suspect some women, including me, stay in marriages because they need financial support, or they don't know how to operate the television. God help us all!

One Thursday night in August, on my early evening walk in the park, I hear what I call folk music. I change my usual walking pattern to get closer to the music. The music is coming from outside the boathouse. I join the circle of dancers doing a Tarantella, an Italian dance I did with my boyfriend Tyrone at Saint Paul's School in fifth grade. I'm no longer a Diva in the nineties, I'm back in New York in the fifties.

All of a sudden, Julian enters the circle of dancers. I didn't see him enter the park.

"Listen, I had to leave the cafe before you came back from your phone call the other day. My wife saw me leave you a note. She is jealous of you, always suspicious that I'm in love with you."

"Are you in love with me, Julian?"

"My God you are such a Diva, a real prima donna. By that I mean you are a strong woman. What will you do next, my darling? I heard about your divorce. I am not as brave as you, I can't afford to get a divorce," he says, as he kisses me goodbye. I go back to the Tarantella, returning to the fifties—a time less complicated than the nineties.

4

Birth of a Teen Diva

The fifties gave me something to push against. Without something to push against, I would never have become the Diva I am today. It was the move from New Jersey to New York in my early teens that changed my life dramatically.

Veronica married Sam, and I became a big sister to two step-brothers and two more brothers within a few years. Can you imagine going from being an only child to having four siblings in a short time? I loved my new life, mainly because our mother was too busy to be obsessed with me.

When I was a child, an outside observer might have described me as a *brat*, a term sometimes used to describe a young Diva. I contradict anyone who aligns brat with Diva. A Diva is a girl or a woman who has a mind of her own, but I did always feel a crown sitting securely on my head. Years later, my friend Julian bought me a crown soon after I married Anthony and moved to Denver.

When Julian, the ultimate bad boy, and I get back together at my ex-husband Anthony's company party, I expect he will pamper me and resurface my bad girl side.

"You're here! Did you get the note I left in the cafe a couple of weeks ago? You know, as I look at you tonight, I wish I had been the first boy to fall in love with you. Tell me about your first boyfriend."

"I was all of eleven years old when my neighbor Johnny fell for me. Johnny came to my backyard with his grandmother's diamond ring, got down on one knee, and asked me to marry him. He claimed his grandparents got engaged when they were twelve, just one year older than us. Besides the fact Johnny never tucked his shirt into his pants, and rarely washed his shaggy long hair, I really wasn't into him."

Roberta Flack's voice fills the room. Julian sings her sensual lyrics as he pulls me closer to him on the dance floor. I can still feel his body next to mine.

"Oh my God, Diane, that was 1953 when Johnny brought you a diamond. You were an emerging Diva then. Just the thought of you in a little poodle skirt is turning me on. You still have some of that eleven-year-old spunkiness in you. I'm so attracted to you right now. Meet me at the Brown Palace for a nightcap," he says, putting his hand on my butt.

I have to leave the party early to pick up a friend at the airport. I knew I would end up doing more than drinking with Julian at the hotel that night. As I drive to the airport, I look back on my responses to boyfriends in the fifties. I see my early flirtations with boys. I was showing my nascent Diva-ness that would later come into bloom in more complicated and elaborate ways.

In fifth grade, I had my first steamy relationship. Tyrone was kind of like the character Fonzie Fonzarelli on *Happy Days*, a popular TV series in the sixties—not squeaky clean, kind of a rebel with slick, dark hair. Tyrone was young but he knew all the right moves, seducing me like a guy in his twenties. I remember him promising someday he would pick me up on a black motorcycle, wearing his signature black leather jacket.

I can still feel Tyrone's rough hands on me forty-two years later. He liked it when my lacy pink panties got wet. If I stained his tight-fitting pants, he said everyone would know he was a real turn-on. The night would typically end with Tyrone having my cherry red lipstick all over his face and I could smell his stale, musky cologne all over my body. Things became complicated one night when Tyrone's sister put moves on me. Before I knew what was happening, his sister pulled me off his lap, flipped me on the grass, and grabbed my sheer white blouse, exposing my breasts. Tyrone ran to me and covered me with his leather jacket. Then he got into a fist fight with his sister.

My early sexual encounters in the fifties were ahead of my time, maybe even considered wild for my age. Actually, the way I lived my life throughout that decade was kind of wild. It may not look wild today, but it did in the mid-fifties.

Looking back on my new life with my mother, stepfather, and two step-brothers seemed fairly normal compared to living in Jersey City. I just wasn't used to things being normal. I missed the dysfunction of my old life; there were no more drunks to entertain in New York.

While I was experiencing the transition from the trauma of my early years to kind of a false innocence as a preteen, in a sense, I was also rebelling against the era and the Catholic Church. For example, I threatened to report Sister Cecilia to our priest at Saint Paul's Middle School because she was always picking on Tyrone. He was an altar boy, for God's sake.

Sister Cecilia, who looked like a mean old owl with her pointed beak of a nose, beaded red-rimmed dark brown eyes, rough dry skin, and split lips, symbolized the inflexibility of the church. She often called me a *smart ass* in nun language. Sometimes Sister Cecilia snorted and farted, making no apologies for the obvious smell between us. I could not stop laughing when the perfectionistic nun made a fool of herself.

This morning I watched the constantly frustrated Sister Cecilia pick Tyrone up by the scruff of his neck, hauling him off to detention because he sang a line of "Little Bitty Pretty One" to me on the way to class. I thought for sure Tyrone would get away with a little misconduct because he didn't mean any harm. Maybe he was a target because his sister was kicked out of Saint Paul's because she was caught kissing a girl on the playground. In the end, my chat with our priest gave Tyrone a reprieve from Sister Cecilia's vengeance. Tyrone and I got away with making out on the playground for over a month without any trouble then.

It's not just the church that imposes a strictness, at home there's a military vibe, too. My natural Diva style is cramped as Veronica and Sam, my new stepfather, transition from the trauma of the forties into the fifties. My father Robert was killed in Germany and my stepfather Sam was injured in Italy during World War II. My parents were into President Eisenhower, who they felt saved the country from communism. His famous quote was taped on our white GE refrigerator. I have to look at it from the kitchen table. Sometimes my brothers and I have to read the quote out loud after we say grace. *Neither a wise man nor a brave man lies down on the tracks of history to wait for the train of the future to run over him.*

Maybe it was the strictness of the fifties that caused Veronica to fixate on putting me in an all-girl Catholic academy, which I called a military school. I had trouble with the nuns in middle school and I expected it to be worse in high school. I don't know what I would have done without my brother Jack, who was my sidekick. Jack had the smoothest, golden hair. It looked like it had been bleached by the sun. He wore it long as a preteen. As Jack got older, Veronica called him a hippy. Jack covered for me when I wanted to run off with one of my boyfriends or when we both needed to sneak cigarettes at Lake Park. A Diva needs a good sidekick like Jack.

It's March 1957. I'm watching my mother fix my favorite pancakes in an outfit that looks like she's going for a job interview in her coral, gaberdine business suit. Veronica usually wore an ugly bathrobe and pink curlers in her hair to breakfast. I knew something was up.

"You're going to the Academy next fall, Diane. Sister Cecilia called me again last night. We agree you are too wild to go to a public high school. Actually, she said if you were her daughter, she would tie you up somewhere. She called you a 'boy crazy Diva,' always the center of attention in your classes."

"Come on, Mom. Sister Cecilia just likes to pick on me because I'm not afraid to stand up to her. Besides, all the nuns are nervous this week because Cardinal Spellman is coming to dedicate the school library. He is, after all, in line to be Pope someday."

After our discussion about whether or not I would go to a private high school, I head for the basement, my go-to place when I have to study for a test. I burrow my back into the pillows on the old couch Addie left us after she died. She liked to sleep down here when she came here to put herself back together when her diabetes got serious. It's a quiet night until our neighbor's collie, Boots, barks just about the time I see a man's face peeking through the crack in the shuttered window in front of me. There's something familiar about the man's face, besides the undeniably sad eyes. It's the creepy priest, Father Damian! I pick up an index card with Sister Cecilia's personal telephone number. She arrives outside our house just a few minutes before the cops show up. One of the neighbors must have called them because Father Damian looked filthy and very disoriented, not a typical visitor in our quiet, slightly upscale neighborhood.

Sister puts her arm around me, probably trying to look human in front of the cops. She explains to them that Father Damian is being sent to a retirement home in another state. He needs to get proper psychological help.

"Okay, Sister, I remember Father Damian," one of the cops says. "He was my history teacher in high school. Why don't I put him in a small room next to my office for a couple of nights? He can stay there until you put him on a plane. Too bad, he has never been quite the same since he was accused of molesting an altar boy. I really don't think he would do something like that," says one of the cops.

After the cops and the priest leave, Sister concludes Father Damian must have followed us home from Saint Paul's that afternoon. After she blesses me with the sign of the cross, Sister Cecilia hands me a picture of Saint Joan of Arc, who she says was brave like me. I carry this image with me years later when I travel to Rouen, in northern France, where Joan of Arc was burned at the stake for defending her town.

I see my family returning with a couple quarts of ice cream. My brother Jack asks why I'm holding one of his baseball bats. They all wonder why Sister Cecilia is here.

The incident seems like a perfect opportunity to plead my case about the dangers of being in a Catholic school, but clearly I was never going to have a say in the decision. Veronica is determined to keep me under control. I had to pay the high tuition for the Academy out of my personal inheritance from my first father. The money didn't come out of Veronica's pocket.

The only thing that saves me the summer before my freshman year at the Academy is meeting up with Tyrone again who dropped out of middle school to work as a trainer at Goodhue Recreation Center. My mother would have freaked out if she knew I was seducing a drop-out. The more Tyrone ignored me at the center, the tighter my pants got. I shrunk my blue jeans by putting them on and laying down in a tub of hot water so when the pants dried they fit my legs like skin. The more I looked like a tart, the more Tyrone and I met to make out in parks, apartment lobbies, and small office buildings. Tyrone walked with a swagger. I loved to mess up his heavily lacquered hair. Being with him was forbidden fun, which is a good way to describe what I sought in the mid-fifties.

The harder it is for my mother to control me, the more abusive she becomes. One Sunday morning, when I refuse to go to church, she throws a hard-heeled loafer at my face, leaving cuts on my nose and forehead. A month later, she sprains my right arm hitting my elbow with the same loafer. When I show up at summer school in a sling, Sister Cecilia calls my mother. Veronica kisses up to her, and, what a surprise, the nun forgets about my injuries. From then on, I never trusted nuns. That was when I started to move away from the Catholic Church. Since I have a self-preservation personality, I know where to draw the line during those rebellious years, taking calculated risks and pushing my boundaries just enough.

I think about Lady Gaga, a famous Diva. She knows if she doesn't maintain her boundaries, she will not be successful. If she were really weird, she wouldn't be the icon she is today. From what I have read, she handled academic life well: a dedicated, studious, and disciplined student. Lady Gaga and I have a few things in common. We were both raised Catholic, went to private, all-girl academies, and we were both sexually abused.

Like Lady Gaga, I've learned to read people and know they are also reading me. I keep myself moving toward success, maintaining my Diva image in my teens. I become a bit of a chameleon when I start high school, pretending to be intellectual in order to fool my mother about how I actually spend my time. I start a book club, which is a cover for me because it gave me a certain image that saved my ass when I just want to spend all my time with boys. It's a challenge because classes at the academy are sans boys.

I use our old attic as a hiding place to pretend I'm reading for a book club that never really meets. The attic is actually where I smoke Marlboros and drink Sam's whiskey. Occasionally my brother Jack joins me for a smoke, if the coast is clear. The attic is completely unfinished, with creaky floors and cheap white shades that bang against the windows. My favorite thing about the attic, besides the fact I can escape there, is my oak trunk with a brass lock and a leather strap across the middle. It's where I store creepy porcelain dolls, a glass ashtray, and *Playboy* magazines. I'm determined to get my photograph in *Playboy* someday. I am developing an intellectual, almost sophisticated, style of making excuses for wrong-doings. Questionable things I do are less suspect because I'm so good at embellishing the truth about things like smoking and having a book club. I'm not Cookie anymore; from now on I want to be called Ginger. I have an attitude, and I'm not putting up with crap!

It's 1957 when I begin my freshman year of high school. I made a real effort to get kicked out right away; I was not cut out to be a good girl. I smoked, drank, cursed, and left the school grounds to make out with boys from the neighboring all-boys Academy. It is mortifying for a Diva like me to ride to school on a public bus in my ugly uniform. I am sure my image is in serious danger. Every morning I alter my look, as if I am preparing for an award-winning performance. I put on a full face of makeup and hike up my long burgundy wool jumper with a wide leather belt. My strappy black heels, black jewelry, and blood-red lipstick finish my look. I am edgy for a girl in the fifties. As soon as I get to school, I have to transform back into looking like a bland school girl. Then, at the end of the day, I repeat my ritual all over again. My father would have been proud of my efforts to maintain my diva image.

I am a show-off in high school. Sometimes I get sent out in the hall for disturbing the peace. I often say something sexually inappropriate in class. I understand now that to be a successful Diva you can't keep getting thrown out of things.

Thank God that Mother Barbara, the principal at the Academy, is the complete opposite of Sister Cecilia at Saint Paul's. Mother is sophisticated. I wonder what she would look like out of her black habit. Every now and then, I can see the tiniest sliver of black hair peeking out from her veil. Mother was both a musician and an artist. Her love of the arts filters into the curriculum at the Academy, which is great for me because I have a creative side too.

Every spring we are forced to be in a concert at Carnegie Hall. There are practices, practices, and more practices.

It is April 1958, my sophomore year. The main thing I remember about the concert is almost getting busted for drinking in the dressing room after the performance. My custom-made, yellow-net gown is draped over a chair. I am standing in my black lace slip, sipping on a shot of whiskey, when I hear someone coming down the hall.

"Holy crap, do you hear the tingling of Rosary beads? Breath mints anyone?" I ask.

Mother came into the dressing room right after we hid the alcohol. She hands out small boxes of her favorite Italian candies as a thank you for our good performance. She didn't seem to care that I am standing around in sexy, black underwear. Mother is more liberal than any nun I have ever met.

After the other girls leave the dressing room, I put a coat over my slip and throw my ugly yellow gown into the dumpster on my way out of Carnegie Hall. I hate yellow. A diva named Ginger doesn't wear an outfit she doesn't like; she's particular.

5

First Love

I meet Bill my sophomore year. His sister, a friend of mine from the alto section, invited me to a party at their house the night after the concert. I am wearing a tight, turquoise, linen skirt with a slit in the front and a matching turquoise, form-fitting, wool sweater. When I catch Bill looking at me as my strappy silver heels move down the steps, I move even more slowly.

"Ginger," Bill says, "dance with me before my heart breaks."

"Watch out, Bill, I am a real heartbreaker."

The song is Elvis's, "I Want You, I Need You, I Love You." Bill draws me close until our legs link. I feel a surge of energy as Bill thrusts his tongue into my waiting mouth.

By the end of the night my lips look as if I have rubbed them with sandpaper. I can't eat for days. This is the first time I have actually fallen in love; I walk around the Academy in a daze.

Bill and I date on and off for almost two years. After six months, he wants me to wear a small, gold friendship ring. He is really asking me to go steady. Going steady in the fifties means being exclusive. My girlfriends say if Bill and I became exclusive, he will take liberties with me. I am already used to boys taking liberties. I like them touching me. I am just not interested in being exclusive. Bill and I exchange wallet-sized photos, and I continued to circulate at social events, playing the field. My parents love that I'm mostly dating Bill because he is 100% Irish.

My stepfather, Sam, often mentions that half his ass got shot off in Italy in the war. I sense it was Sam's war experience that made him cautious about Italians. There was a kind of long-standing rivalry between the Irish and the Italians on the East Coast in the fifties. Both cultures have Catholicism in common. Apparently, not enough to bond the two ethnicities. The Irish feel threatened by what they perceive as competition coming from the struggling Italians, who can barely make enough money to put food on the table. Their struggle to survive leads to brawls and street fights in New York. *Brooklyn,* a nostalgic movie from 2015 produced in the UK, is about Rose, a young Irish immigrant struggling to navigate her way through American culture in the fifties.

All of this prior knowledge of the Irish struggle helps me make sense of why Christmas of 1959 could have been a total disaster if Bill hadn't been Irish.

My home in New York is a two-story, white, colonial-style house—perfect to decorate for Christmas. The tree is scattered with vintage ornaments, candle lights, and strung popcorn with cranberries. The dining room smells like a combination of fresh pine and cinnamon sticks. It's my senior year of high school.

It is turning dark when carolers arrive on our front porch to sing "Hark! The Herald Angels Sing." I finish decorating the sugar cookies before getting ready for my date with Bill. It is a home date. Veronica is sure I'm catching a cold, so we don't go out. I wear a new mint green and light pink wool outfit, an early Christmas gift.

Bill arrives at midnight on Christmas Eve. The living room is dark except for the Santa Claus and snowman candles burning next to a dish of Christmas cookies. Bill and I make out on the persimmon silk couch in the living room, a piece Veronica had acquired before the holidays. While Bill grabs another beer, I move the candles to the Art Deco table by the couch, not noticing they are dripping all over the beige wall-to-wall carpet.

As soon as Bill comes back from the kitchen, we resume making out. I love his style of kissing: rough, intentional, yet slow paced. I want to have sex with him.

Maybe I thought my pussy was smoking, because I don't notice that Bill's cigarette has fallen off the ashtray and is burning a large hole in one of the cushions on the new couch. Bill puts his Marlboro out as I wave my hands around to redistribute the smoke and spray my mother's pine air freshener all over the downstairs. Neither Bill or I notice the mess of melted wax on the carpet. *Veronica will never know*, I say to myself as I ask God for forgiveness before I turn the cushion to the good side.

Truthfully, if Bill hadn't burned a hole in the couch, I might have had sex with him, ended up getting pregnant, and living in a convent in Canada waiting for my baby to be born, only to be put up for adoption. This actually happened to two of my girlfriends, and it wasn't going to happen to me. Even if good birth control had been available in the fifties, Catholic girls were forbidden to use any protection except the rhythm method, which really didn't work.

I get up early on Christmas Day to check on the damage from the night before. Since my brothers are not allowed to open presents until after church, I feel that if I play my mother's favorite Christmas songs, I might avoid a scene until after Mass. Veronica loves Christmas songs because they remind her of the crazy holidays in Jersey City. She never really cottoned to Staten Island; it was too slow for her. It was slow for me, too. I missed being able to perform.

When we return from Christmas Mass, Veronica sees the melted wax on the living room carpet. Lucky for me, she waits until the next day to deal with the situation. Oh my God, I watch my mother put waxed paper on top of the wax, and iron the waxed paper to remove the wax. Instead, she burns a hole in the middle of the carpet.

For some odd reason, Veronica handles the situation well, only grounding me for a couple of days. Was it because she didn't mind getting new carpet or was it because she knew I would be going away to college soon?

I don't date Bill the rest of my senior year, mainly because he is drinking more. He starts spending more time in pubs with the guys rather than spending time with me. Plus, I need to concentrate on getting into college.

My mother is hell-bent on sending me out of New York. A friend of hers mentioned WVU in Morgantown, West Virginia. Veronica loves the 9 p.m. curfews. She's convinced I will stay out of trouble there, perhaps even become a lady.

Speaking of becoming a lady, Veronica is thrilled when Mother Barbara requires me to attend Miss Rose's Charm School. Miss Rose, my guide to becoming charming, is on a mission to help us Academy girls find a good man. That thought still makes me gag. Dream on, Miss Rose, I'm not in a hurry!

I learn to walk like a model, how to choose the right outfits to attract a man, and how to set a proper table. Obviously, I know how to dress. I have Diva in my blood. Why would I ever give a damn about a salad fork ending up on the right side of the plate rather than on the left? I never plan to set a fancy table on my own. I expect to be rich enough to have a maid take care of those details. The charm school is a joke, but I did like Miss Rose. Let's face it: walking around with a book on my head to improve my posture is better than sitting through Latin 4, which I know will never be of value in the real world.

My strongest memory of Charm School is of the night I dropped a meatball on my certificate of completion. Although my mother doesn't notice whether I became particularly charming, she did frame my meatball-stained certificate, which she proudly displayed in the kitchen.

After graduating with honors from the Academy, I was set to go to WVU because, once again, my mother held strong to the fact that I needed control. Veronica never really trusted me, nor did she understand my ardent desire for fame and wealth would keep me out of serious trouble.

Before college, I take typing classes at Katherine's School of Business. The required business attire, which included long, white gloves, fed into my Diva style. Everyone at Katherine's looked sickeningly wealthy. I didn't mind the pretense and believed that learning business skills would develop another side of my Diva-ness.

At the same time, I was working on my naughty Diva style, never forgetting my desire to be in *Playboy*. One Saturday afternoon, after I decline taking a ride to the Jersey Shore for what my family called a *shore dinner*, I seduce a photographer friend of mine to do naughty photos of me. I wear different pieces of lingerie, mostly Veronica's sheer nightgowns designed by my Aunt Iris who had become a famous designer in the early fifties. I plan to submit these Polaroids to *Playboy*.

My mother finds the risqué Polaroids after I'm in college, right around the time she finds Bill's burn hole in the living room cushion. *Double trouble*, I think! Surprisingly, Veronica forgives me because my narcissistic roommate is all I can deal with at WVU in the fall of 1959.

When I was at the university, I wrote a few reflections about the vaguely-defined figure I perceived as my mother. I was actually starting to see her in myself. She had a creative side, nurtured by my uncle William, an architect and designer. When Veronica was stuck in the past, she was not only sad, she was mean. The more time Veronica spent working in my uncle's design studio, the better life became for me. It's not until years later, after my divorce from Anthony, that my mother is finally proud of me. She applauded my decision to get a master's degree in art and psychology, acknowledging my academic success and the goals I set. It's sad some mothers take so long to acknowledge the achievements of their daughters.

My family wasn't rich, but I thought of myself as rich. Veronica made sure I wore expensive clothes. She ironed my labels: from Saks Fifth Avenue, Lord & Taylor, and others. No one ever saw my labels, but she ironed them anyway. She never gave up her fear that my father's family would take me away from her. The facade of making me look wealthy and pampered continued until I was eleven.

Everything changed when a family member, probably Uncle Frank, gave me a bike. From the first time I got on my Schwinn, I knew I was not going to put up with Veronica's craziness anymore. No more being mean to me. No more keeping me home from school when I wasn't sick. One way or another, I was going to get away from the house of drunks and become the famous Diva I was meant to be.

6

Freedom

Freedom is not being for or against an ideal, but creating your own existence from scratch.
—Glennon Doyle

Today, some thirty years after the night I met my husband Anthony, I am a free, single woman in my mid-fifties, enjoying a new life.

It's a magnificent, or possibly spectacular, day in my neighborhood close to the city. My new home is just fifteen minutes from lower downtown Denver. I'm close to the Denver Art Museum, the Botanical Gardens, the famous Cherry Creek Mall, and a large selection of restaurants and bars. It's like living back in New York. I love being a city girl again. I'm an autonomous Diva, free of the chains of being in a controlling marriage. I am sharpening my charms as I get rid of my old tapes about how a middle-aged woman should act. No one has the right to tell me how I should express my feelings or who to love.

All of this scintillating energy gives me what Veronica referred to as my *strong body urges.* I've been sexually deprived in a marriage with a man who felt that anything other than the missionary position was a sin.

I've been blessed with a lovely guide and personal friend in my psychic, Dora. Sometimes it feels as if we're wired together. On the drive up from Denver to Dora's house, I feel melancholic, confused, maybe even a little lonely. I pull up to her large, contemporary home in the foothills west of Boulder. I attempt to knock on her door, which she opens before my knuckles can strike the wood.

"Congratulations on your divorce, Diane. You're free now! You mentioned on the phone you're ready to start dating. Remember this, dear, nothing uproots anyone's life more than falling in love. I suggest you fall in love with sex again. I love my vibrator called the Beaver. If you like, I can give you information on ordering one," Dora says, fanning herself.

A big black and white poodle enters the room. He's Moby, perhaps named after Moby Dick. Moby lays at my feet as I snuggle up on the leather couch with one of Dora's luscious, gray, cashmere throws. I pull the blanket to my chin as the snow starts to fall, making me anxious about the drive home tonight.

When Dora sees I'm fixated on the large picture windows, she lets me know I can stay with her tonight. My body relaxes as Dora pours Earl Grey tea from a royal purple ceramic teapot into matching tea cups. She tells me I must sip this tea very slowly and pay attention to the after-taste. I feel balmy as the tea opens up my unconscious, giving me clarity as Dora predicted would happen. Before taking a seat diagonally across from me, Dora looks at me with compassionate eyes and says, "I hope you know how much I care about you, Diane."

It occurs to me that anyone who truly gets us and sees us is a gift, giving us a feeling of unconditional love. We all need to be mirrored, even an outrageous Diva like me. Without somebody loving us, we are left to crawl out of life's deepest holes alone.

Maybe one of the hard things about being a Diva is being alone. Divas are provocative, different, and sometimes at odds with the mainstream.

People are fascinated by us. They wish they were like us, sometimes wishing they could be so entertaining, but they rarely dare to get close to us. Most people who live in their carefully constructed boxes are unable to see us for who we are. We scare them sometimes. Divas live in a Catch-22. We have to be ourselves. We can't live false lives to please others. I've known for years the cost of being myself can be high because we often threaten the status quo. Ultimately, we have to find the people who love us. We have to love ourselves. Dora is here to show me how.

After a wonderful evening of conversation, Dora shows me to my room, which is warm and lovely. I immediately feel I'm in my home away from home. Dora brings me a kimono like the one I tried on in her office. She hands me a vial of essential oils meant to heal childhood wounds. My new journal from her is inscribed with *Do not fear the challenges you are facing. You wouldn't be taking them if you weren't ready. Have faith in your progress.*

I flop onto the bed, exhausted. Moby makes himself comfortable at the bottom of the bed. I look out the window, noticing a doe meandering across the field. Moby jumps farther up on the bed as I climb under the heavily tufted covers. Dora wishes us both pleasant dreams as she mentions Moby loves the particular smell of my healing herbs.

"Sleep well tonight, my dears," she says, patting Moby on the head.

Most of the time, I feel good about how my body looks, at least superficially. I don't think too hard about my scars from breast surgery. I think of myself as a young Diva with a perfect body. Sometimes I wish I could go back in time. I wonder what I would look like dressed in loincloths, like the Roman goddess Artemis, known in Greece as Diana, my namesake. My body trembles as I bring up this old myth about a goddess who cut off her right breast so she could use her bow and arrow more efficiently.

Artemis, goddess of the hunt, is represented as an earthy, powerful Diva. She shows me being a Diva can be more about power than anything else. Divas identify themselves in many ways.

Dora comes back into the room one more time and puts her strong arms around me, causing me to cry deep sobs, snot running out of my nose. I'm sure my eyes are puffy. I feel like running out of Dora's front door as fast as I can. Dora pours a shot of whiskey for me before I can even get out from under the covers.

I watch the snow continue to fall, leaving its sparkle on the tall pine trees. Dora must have slipped out of the room when I dozed off. I wake up at six the next morning. I see what I was too exhausted to see last night: the walls in the bedroom are the color of melted butter, making me feel warm as the sun rises. There are collections of old crystals, fossils, and shells in glass cases at the bottom of the bed. I pick up one tagged *topaz*. The back of the tag reads: *abundance of life, the joy of the heart.*

Moby is getting restless. I write down a few words from my dream last night. The two of us head out the back door into the crisp air, fresh after last night's snowstorm. A black crow flies past Moby, landing on a small branch jutting out of the snow. It's as if the bird is posing for us. I guess a crow can be a Diva too. Moby observes the crow making no attempt to chase him. When the dog tires of watching the bird, he sticks his snout into the snow and we both return to the house.

Dora is waiting for me with a cup of coffee. After we share a light breakfast of fruit and yogurt, she suggests we write for thirty minutes. "Feel free to write down any dreams from last night," she says.

1995. Remembering a dream:

I see myself in a light blue dress with a lace collar and long, white socks, secured at the knees with blue satin ribbons. My feet are stuffed into white Mary Jane shoes, not my favorites because they're too tight. My blue straw hat feels scratchy against my face. I look about eight years old in the dream. My long red curls swirl below the hat. I imagine my hair full of pink curlers the night before. I see my mother pull out a brass settee from our bedroom. She places it in front of the three glass windows in the living room. There is just enough sunlight for a good photo. I'm holding a small, purple basket filled with raw eggs, not boiled, not colored, just white and uncooked.

"Smile! Say cheese, Cookie! We can frame this photo and put it next to your Christmas picture with Blackie," my Mother grins.

"You mean Blackie, the puppy Pop gave me, my first pet, the one you got rid of right after Christmas?" I hear myself say.

My grandmother, Addie, is smoking a long cigarette as she pours oil into a frying pan. She sets the cigarette down on the right side of the gas stove, which Veronica tells her could start a fire. Addie must not be going to church on Easter because she is wearing one of her nasty, faded house dresses. I watch her crack my eggs into the hot frying pan.

Veronica yells at Addie, "Mom, no one likes ashes in their eggs. Put the cigarette out in this ashtray right now." Addie slops the fried eggs onto chipped porcelain plates she claims belonged to her mother, who brought the plates to New Jersey from Ireland. Special Easter bread is placed on each plate with the eggs. The smell of coffee fills the kitchen.

"Pop, can we pick some flowers along the way to church for the statue of Saint Theresa?" I hear myself ask in what my family calls my Cookie voice.

"Sure," he says. "Maybe Saint Theresa will talk to the Easter Bunny on your behalf. You're such a good girl, Cookie!"

"The Easter Bunny never comes to our house, Pop, because the Easter Bunny isn't real. You think I'm a good girl because you feel so happy when you bounce me on your knee."

Pop looks sad and a little scared. His face has a kind of innocence about it in the dream which, of course, I can't decipher at such a young age.

Later, Veronica comes into the kitchen wearing her spring coat, a cream-colored soft long coat with big brass buttons. Her straw hat is decorated with rose-colored flowers, she made herself. Pop, Veronica, and I walk to Saint Anne's church. Mass has already started when we arrive. I run down the aisle toward the statue of Saint Theresa, my favorite saint. My mother's face is turning red as she motions for me to come back to the pew. I ignore her; I need time with the saint.

"Saint Theresa, I want a new father who will take me away from Pop. Please help me." I pray.

I see a tall usher coming toward me. Veronica signals—I belong to her. Pop gives me a thumbs up but we both know my mother isn't happy.

When the writing is finished Dora hands me a terry-cloth robe for the outside sauna. The warmth of the sauna hits me fast after trudging through the snow to get there. The "no self-criticism" rule Dora has in place for sharing personal writing opens me up to speak freely. Dora pours eucalyptus oil and water on the rocks, adding moisture to the sauna as I share my thoughts about last night's dream. Which, in my opinion, hints at Pop's subtle inappropriate behavior toward me at a young age.

"Remember, Diane, there are no special formulas for interpreting dreams. Record even the simplest ones as often as you can. Pay attention to how you feel in the dream. You are the expert here. Dreams heal us without too much effort on our part," she says.

The dream shows me my mother was interested in having me pose as a happy-five-year-old girl on Easter, which was not the kind of Easter every little girl dreams of. The raw, uncolored Easter eggs ended up in a frying pan, allowing me to see Addie as a rather odd, unstable woman in last night's dream.

I can also see Pop doing something wrong when he bounces me on his knee. It makes me want to reach out to that little girl within me who still feels guilty about not speaking up about her grandfather. Not even a year later, I'm more sure Pop is doing something wrong because after he bounces me on his knee, he leaves to use the bathroom and returns with stains on the front of his pants because he didn't make it to the bathroom before he came.

"Your thoughts on the dream are both knowing and powerful. Stay longer in the sauna, Diane, take your time, breathe in love, breathe out fear. Continue to write. Don't be surprised if you surface a connection between being molested and some of your struggles with body image you mentioned last night and possibly your attraction to men who you call *bad boys*. You might also be able to connect your grandfather's sexual abuse to getting breast cancer later in life. Drink plenty of water please. You're cleansing old memories."

As I stand in front of the mirror in the sauna, I wince a little, a swamp of confusion comes over me, probably because I have kept so many feelings about my body inside. I watch myself examine the tiny scars above my breasts with sweaty hands, remembering what I experienced when plastic surgeons dropped implants into my breast flaps, which were minus most of my breast tissue. The left breast was full of cysts, making it a wise decision to remove the tissue, according to my male doctors who apparently didn't think it mattered I would lose most of the feeling in the breast that wasn't cancerous.

The scars I have from breast reconstruction look like white polka dots, which stand out this morning because I have some tan left over from summer. My breasts look firm, and they'll remain that way for the rest of my life.

"My body is beautiful!" I say out loud as I make a decision to rid my mind of any of my ex-husband's negative remarks about me post-cancer. I recall a quote by Estee Lauder: "Beauty is an attitude. There is no secret." My thin body is speckled with tiny droplets of sweat, giving it a light gloss. Breathe in love, breathe out fear. I'm falling in love with myself.

Dora and I finish this visit by sipping glasses of Champagne as we take turns reading verses of a poem from "Leaves of Grass" by Walt Whitman. "I breathe the fragrance of myself. I know it and I like it," I read.

Dora runs out to the car as I start to leave the canyon. "On your way home, think about a time, preferably in your childhood or in your early teens, when you felt free. Write or tape your memories. Talk soon!" she says, with a smile as impressive as her knowing eyes.

I get in my car and head out of the mountains onto the turnpike from Boulder to Denver. I speed up a little and roll down the windows to feel the cool wind blowing my unkempt red hair in my face. The sensation of feeling free takes me back to 1952 when I was just ten years old and gained enough power to fight for my freedom.

It was the day I learned how to ride my bike and somehow knew I was going to move out of Jersey City soon. Like Dora, I was born with an intuitive nature. I saw my new turquoise Schwinn as a symbol of getting out of the house of drunks.

A memory comes in as I continue driving.

It was early Monday morning when Uncle Frank came by to give me the brand new turquoise Schwinn, along with a card that explained everything I needed to know about the Panther, as it was called. White wall tires, chrome-plated fenders, and a chrome-plated tank. This Model D-27 had a horn, a three-speed hub, and a light. I loved the long, slinky kickstand and the handlebar, which Frank covered with pink and white rabbit's feet for good luck.

Since it was my first time on a bike, I wobbled a little as I got ready to launch my escape out of the neighborhood. "You can do this, Cookie, don't be afraid. Remember the first time you sang like Shirley Temple on New Year's Eve? You were a great little performer. How about you give me a bike song to go with the ride?" Pop said.

Pop must have known about the bike and probably let Frank in while he got ready for work. Thank God Veronica was still asleep when the two men got the bike out of the box and out of the house.

Pop came down later wearing his J. C. Penney's gray suit, white shirt, navy tie, and dress shoes. I'm sure he had his Celtic flask full of Irish whiskey in the briefcase he was carrying.

"Salesman of the Year for Swift and Company," he would say when he was drunk. I can remember a look of concern on his face when he warned me to ride the bike on the sidewalk. The minute he drove off, Frank, my friend Johnny, and I took the bike into the middle of Thorne Street. Once Frank saw me pedaling as fast as I could, with my friend Johnny running right beside me, he got in his car, planning to go back home. I figure he knew Veronica would be yelling from the porch any minute, and there she was with her hair in curlers standing barefoot in a pair of baby-doll pajamas.

Frank got out of his car and put his left arm around Veronica's waist, hoping to buy me more time.

"Diane, you get in the house right now or you're going to be grounded for a week! Bring me that damn bike!"

I look at my mother, knowing her raised fist means she is going to try to hurt me when she gets me back to 116 Thorne Street. I'm not afraid of Veronica's punishment because I know she can't really hurt me anymore. She will get in trouble if she tries. I have decided to report her to my teacher, or I will ride my Schwinn to the police station. The marks on my body will prove my mother hurts me.

"No, come and get me!" I said as I moved the pedals even faster. My red hair was surely blowing in the wind as the rabbit's feet were clicking on the handle bar, causing every dog in the neighborhood to bark. Some followed me. My friend Johnny was singing "God Bless America" as he ran beside me. We made it all the way to Richmond Avenue, fifteen blocks away. I proudly parked my Schwinn in front of the corner bakery. Johnny watched the bike while I got jelly donuts and two big glasses of water.

Johnny, soaking wet, gulped the water down before he could even speak. The red jelly oozed out of my mouth and made a big smear above my upper lip. I remember thinking Johnny was my superhero, saving his damsel in distress that day. He'd had a crush on me since we were little kids. "Take my biggest rabbit's foot, Johnny, the black one. Wear it for good luck. It was good to have you along for the ride!" I said.

There was something about getting far from Thorne Street that let me begin to understand I was free now. Veronica, because of her own fear issues and insecurity, kept me in a type of quarantine the first eleven years of my life. The truth is: my mother was only nice to me when I was sick or when she convinced herself I was sick. Was she was afraid of losing me or was she just mentally ill?

Veronica looked distraught in her beautiful red dress, probably because she broke one of her red heels running after me. Her hair was a mess from running in the heat when she finally caught up with Johnny and me. I couldn't help laughing at my mother's dilemma. She looked pathetic, thumping around on one foot—plus she had to know she would never truly hold me in her clutches easily again.

The Schwinn was stuck in the backyard shed for a week. Johnny would sneak me punks to smoke at night. We watched fireflies circle around us, me on the steps of the front porch and him on the sidewalk. One night a firefly attached itself to my hair. Johnny said it was magic. I set the firefly free, but in my imagination it stayed with me, lighting up the yellow bedroom with the big, white flowers before I slept.

Remembering a combination of getting my Schwinn bike, standing up to Veronica, and knowing one way or another I was going to get out of a toxic home, affirmed the decision I made to get out of a toxic marriage. All of those experiences gave me the gravitas to consider dating, which I hadn't done since I was in my early twenties.

7

Romance

Before I start dating, I revert back to a style of dress I wore in the late eighties. I call the style *punk meets disco*. I must be taking on a Dora look since I've been around her so much. My closet is full of long skirts in Granny-Smith green and brick red, black and white embroidered peasant tops, long velvet coats, and tall boots in earthy colors. The shopping malls are too boring for me now. My outfits come from small boutiques from different parts of the country. My early single life gives me a new nickname: Gypsy.

When I travel, I look for small hotels with interesting architecture. I am an historian and a nomad exploring different parts of the city, gallivanting with a purpose. I drive to Santa Fe on long weekends, returning with crystals, African masks, Spanish crosses, colorful beads, and fresh sage to purify my new home.

After I get my fill of traveling and collecting, I am ready to start dating.

Romance ads, a popular alternative to online dating in the nineties, take up a large section of my favorite local paper, *Westword*. The process of meeting men becomes like a business for me. I can access messages sent from the paper to my answering machine easily without the caller knowing any personal information about "Vibrant Redhead."

"Good morning, you sound like fun. I have a degree in mechanical engineering with a specialty in designing rockets. In my spare time I play the piano, go to fine restaurants, and visit museums all over the world. I'm GQ handsome!"

I nickname this caller GQ. After a couple of conversations, I realize the only thing true about GQ is that he's a mechanical engineer. I put him down as a *maybe*.

Some callers accuse me of interrogating them. Damn right. I'm a particular Diva. I admit I am a skilled interviewer, relying mainly on my ability to figure out personality types using the Enneagram, an ancient Sufi personality study that originated in the Middle East, about two-thousand years ago. It became a western psychological tool in the thirties. Some of the early western books on the Enneagram were written by Jesuit priests.

After listening to at least ten calls in a week, I agree to a meet up with David, who I nickname Renaissance Man because he seems to be romantic, creative, and not narcissistic like many of the men who have answered my ad.

I watch David open the door of a small cafe in the neighborhood. He looks as if he isn't sure if he wants to enter or not. He pauses for a minute, scanning the restaurant for me. David looks between twelve and fifteen years younger than me. Seeing David dressed in a business suit seems out of character for a cafe on a Saturday in Denver. I'd expected he would wear casual clothes since he was a professional baseball player in the day. Everyone else, including myself, is wearing casual clothes. Maybe he just wants to make an impression on me. I did describe myself as a Diva in my "Vibrant Redhead" ad.

After a few minutes of conversation, I can tell David is intelligent and well-read. I think he's sexy, in an intellectual sort of way. Is David one of those complicated, quiet men who keeps everything inside? I must admit his fixation on me is both surprising and stimulating for an introverted observer. When he puts his hand on his forehead to fan back a section of his blond hair, I can see his probing blue eyes looking at my lips as I slowly part them. When David mentions the title of my ad, he insinuates the word "vibrator." I lick my lips just to tease him.

David asks to meet him for dinner later that week. I tell him I'll get back to him. It was his extreme shyness and frequent trips to the men's room the day we met that concern me.

A week later, I stop at the same cafe where David and I met. "Pumpkin almond latte with extra cinnamon and nutmeg," I say to the brewster as I enjoy the hissing sound of the steamer.

The owner's wife stops by my table with a white orchid and a card from David. *I want you to be my rare orchid. Give me another chance! David.*

I knew "Renaissance Man" was the appropriate moniker for him. When I call David to thank him for the gift, he insists we need to meet for dinner.

"Why did you call me a *rare orchid*, David?" I ask.

"Is that a problem, Diane? It was just a gut feeling I had. You are kind of a rare Diva. Orchids are my favorite flower." David's response to my question gets him a formal date with me.

Park Grill is cozy, with brick walls and a small fireplace in the back. A jazz quartet is playing George Benson's "Love Remembers" as I walk toward the corner table in the back.

My Manolo Blahnik black heels give me a seductive Diva look, exposing my legs under a black mini skirt. My white designer tee with *Merci* in black letters written across my chest is a conversation piece. My black hoop earrings accent my short red hair.

"Your legs are so tan for late fall, Diane."

I point to the word Merci on my tee as a way of thanking him, but does he think I'm just pointing out my firm breasts?

I watch David put an ochre hardcopy of *Men Are from Mars, Women Are from Venus* on the table. I read the book, but didn't agree with John Gray that women are demanding and men need to be pampered because of their hormone levels, nevertheless, it is the hottest book on relationships in the nineties.

"Are you actually looking for a relationship, Diane? Because I am!" David starts the conversation tonight.

I laugh because his lack of finesse is almost charming. I plan to enjoy my meal, drink my wine, and listen to the music, so I shrug my shoulders, avoiding an answer. Renaissance Man is a journalist, bridge champion, house painter, and, as he mentioned the last time we met, he was a professional baseball player.

After a nice two-hour dinner, I'm surprised when David suggests we split the check, mentioning it is the nineties, after all. I snicker at him as I put cash on the table and mention I'm a Diva who likes to be treated like a lady. He's cheap I conclude. The truth is, I had enough of that attitude with my husband, Anthony.

Timing is everything in life. I received an invitation to a poetry competition in Paris the day after my date with David. I'm sure my professor friend Charles recommended me for this honor.

My room in the Paris hotel is a classic one, with a mahogany, queen-size bed fit for a queen. There are six tufted, French blue pillows sitting on top of a European-style duvet which is cream with just a hint of daisies in the fabric. The walls are also in cream, surrounded with gold trimmed woodwork. The small working fireplace is made of elaborate white porcelain with an inner lining of soft red brick. I use the small ebony desk next to the fireplace to record my plans for the following day.

The next morning, the birds are in a flutter outside my window, which the French tell me is a sign of good weather. After the maid, dressed in a black formal uniform, greets me with a friendly "bonjour," she places a *petit dejeuner* on the mahogany table by the balcony. I sip my coffee from a small Limoges cup before eating and breathing in the smells of early morning in Paris.

"Madame," the maid says, "you must take a stroll today in one of our parks, or perhaps you would like to visit Montmartre? It's always lively there with street artists and musicians all around."

I add raspberry jam to my croissant, taking one more look at the blue tile rooftops and wondering if I will find love in the City of Love. Before dressing, I douse myself with N'aimez que Moi, a French perfume created in Paris in 1916. I slip into my black pencil skirt and red leather pumps after I feel the softness of my lavender silk blouse touching my skin.

"Looking rather French today, Madame Morrison. Do you realize you have a striking resemblance to our famous singer, the diva Edith Piaf? She started performing when she was seven years old. Unfortunately we lost her more than thirty years ago. Her voice would bring a tear to the most insensitive eye. Piaf had a hard life, ultimately, driven by addiction, but she had an air about her, as do you, madame," the connoisseur says as he blows me a kiss.

I have a strong desire to start singing "La Vie en Rose," Piaf's most famous song. I wonder how she maintained her Diva image throughout a life so full of poverty and pain.

The sky looks heavy now, the color of putty, as I prepare to tour the city while carrying the hotel's signature large black umbrellas. Starting at the D'Orsay Museum, home of the largest collection of impressionist paintings in the world, I linger under the glass ceiling of what used to be a Beaux Art's Rail Station, built in the eighteenth century. I feel as if I'm in a dream as I take in Van Gogh, Monet, Renoir, Manet, and more. When face to face with Van Gogh's sunflowers, I have to stop myself from touching the thick, textured paint. I feel the artist's energy in the Dutch pigments. The tour guide reads a Van Gogh quote as she finishes her charming explanation of the piece: "I am seeking, I am striving, I am in it with all my heart."

I want a man with that kind of passion and openness to the act of creating. There he was—a handsome, charming Frenchman offering me a long-stemmed rose and a La Vien en Rose cocktail.

"Madame Morrison, I enjoyed your combination of painting and reciting poetry for the competition. You are a talented artist. I will be finished working at *dix heures*. I am one of the sommeliers here at the hotel. Would you like to see the wine cellar? Perhaps a bottle of wine?"

Didier returns to my table at exactly the time promised. He and I walk down the thick stone stairs. I inch my cashmere shawl up to cover the front of my sleeveless black dress. The air becomes increasingly cold and damp as we get closer to the cellar, which feels more like a crypt.

Death Is A Mystery by Diane Morrison

I hear the voices of the dead,

I shiver like a child,

Save me from the fear in my head

"Is there anyone buried down here, Didier?" I ask.

"Maybe only my lost dreams," he responds.

I admire Didier's artistic flair, his cropped white tee with large flowers in soft pinks and lime greens which he wears over loose creamy linen pants. It pleases him that I like his look. Apparently his wife feels he looks too feminine. I assure him we are all androgynous.

"Follow me, cheri. Sometimes I store studies purchased at auctions here before I take them home. These studies purchased today remind me of Berthe Morisot's work. You must admire Berthe yourself, because your still life that you presented with your poem has some of Berthe's style: the large brush strokes, the soft color of the grapes, and the feeling that the painting goes past the edge. Morisot and Morrison—perhaps you are Berthe reincarnated. I wish to buy your painting 'Red and Green Grapes' and the poem 'The Girl Who Ate Poisoned Grapes.'"

Didier and I make a strong commitment to stay in touch. Both of us are obsessed with Berthe Morisot, who he again insists I am in another body. I am tempted to tell him about Dora and all of her predictions about me.

While I'm a Diva who would enjoy a little more flirtation with such a charming Frenchman, I have commitments in Denver I can't ignore. Didier and I say our *au revoirs* at Charles De Gaulle Airport the following day.

When I return to Denver, I feel like a new person: perhaps a more pretentious Diva after getting up in front of an audience of strangers to read my poetry, then selling the poem and a painting in Paris.

The only thing that kept my Diva side flourishing from the sixties through the mid-nineties was my admiration for famous Divas, especially those who were well known in the music world, such as Elton John, Mariah Carey, and Sade. I admire Sade because she maintains an image of candidness and yet wears a mask to protect what Jung calls her *persona*. The stakes are getting higher for me as I risk getting below my persona. Who am I as a single woman in my fifties? I feel ready to find out.

In the meantime, my dating craze continues: one date for breakfast, another for lunch, another for dinner. Each experience tells me more about myself, but this is getting exhausting. Bad boys can be a lot of fun, but they're usually not the right pick for a functional, long-term relationship. I know this, but I keep going back for more. Dora suggests I do a little soul-searching.

"Diane, you're addicted to the emotional roller coaster. Can you get your thrills elsewhere?

Dear Ms. Morrison,

On behalf of Colorado University I am pleased to congratulate you on your acceptance into our master's program with a major in visual art and a minor in philosophy. Please find the necessary enrollment form for the spring semester of 1996 which must be returned by December 1, 1995.

Dean of Admissions,

Colorado University

8

Kama Sutra

"David here. Diane, please call me. I would like to deliver an early Christmas present. I'm happy to leave it on your front porch if you like. By the way, I had an HIV test."

Three significant things came into play concerning Renaissance Man. I was getting tired of dating so many different men, wanted to have sex with either an artist or a writer, and David did have an HIV test. Before I return Renaissance Man's phone call, I pick up wine, condoms, and incense at a local grocery store where I run into a colleague. She giggles as she looks at the items in my hand and tells me to have a good weekend in an exaggerated tone.

David arrives with a mixed bouquet of flowers and a black cashmere scarf the next night. First we dance, and as he tightens his hold on me I can smell his shampoo, a combination of green apples and peppermint. When we pause, David shows me his beautiful athletic body in stages. I smooth the hair on his chest as he unbuttons his shirt. When he unbuckles his belt and lets his khaki pants drop to the floor, I note the tightness of his legs.

Sex that night is on the Asian wool rug in the living room. My sounds excite David, sounds he suggests lions might make when they're mating. We sleep until noon the next day. Before the next round of sex, he covers me in lime blossom oil, which he acts as if he carries like other men might carry a white handkerchief.

When David returns from a quick stop at his apartment, he has a change of clothes and a new book, *The Ultimate Kama Sutra Sex Guide*. Is he working on a degree in sex?

We have agreed to be weekend lovers so we have one more night together this weekend. I watch David prepare dinner and notice he cooks like he makes love. He relates to the food, fondling the ingredients, seasons properly, and serves.

When David meets me at the park three days later, I watch him standing by the boathouse, looking more approachable in his jeans and casual jacket. His slicked-back, blond hair looks glossy in the sunlight. A young woman, with long strawberry blond hair and wearing a green costume, is dancing close to where David is standing in front of the boathouse. People walking by her try to shoo her away as if she's a stray dog. A woman walking next to me mentions that Lilly, who she agrees looks like a character in a fairy tale, is mentally ill.

"When it's cold, Lilly lives in a shelter downtown. When it's warm, she lives on the street. Since she doesn't have the grocery cart with her pet goose, today I'll take her to the shelter before someone calls the cops," the woman says.

When I catch up with David, I mention Lilly. He knows her because she comes to the soup kitchen where he volunteers once a week. According to him she was a famous actress on Broadway in the day. Part of me wants to ask David if he has ever lived in a shelter. Before I get a chance, as if he read my mind, he tells me he's a creative man who prefers to live outside the box, does travel, sometimes camps out, but has never lived in a shelter.

After David hands me a small bottle of Champagne in a brown paper bag, he invites me to look through *The Ultimate Kama Sutra Sex Guide* while we sit in a secluded garden in the center of the park. "Kama Sutra is a Hindu guide to the three purposes of life: religion or *Dharma*, worldly success or *Artha*, and pleasure or *Karma*. Should we try this one first after I move in next Friday night?" he says, as if this position will be the first in a series.

The following weekend, the kitchen is full of the smell of turkey, stuffing, mashed potatoes, and fresh green beans when I arrive home from school the weekend before Christmas break. I prepare the table with colorful linens, French plates, crystal stemware, and sterling silver tableware, recalling what I learned from Miss Rose's Charm School at the Academy. I knew proper manners would come in handy someday.

David finishes the table with a vase of white roses. He kisses me for a long time. I'm not sure if we'll make it through the meal without having sex. I love the way my seductive side has free reign with him. He calls me a primitive lover. Being involved with a young, sexy man like David makes me feel like a young Diva, the one that had plans to be in *Playboy*.

David continues to be my weekend lover, a perfect living arrangement because I'm busy teaching and working on my master's degree. Reflecting back on our time together, I wonder why a couple of years later I chose to marry again. A weekend lover was just what an adventurer like me needs.

Lucky for me, David is taking an interest in fixing up my house. We visit antique stores, consignment shops, and buy decorative sheets that become window treatments, ethnic scarves that become table runners, old lamps he rewires and stains with deep copper colors. When he restores an antique walnut armoire, David begins to bring more clothes to the house and the weekend stays are four nights now instead of two. Eventually he paints all of the walls using French creams, yellows, and blues. He moves the furniture around, we add interesting old clocks, large candle holders, vases, and other accessories to the decor.

David is an addicted reader as well as a writer. One evening he brings a half-dozen beautifully illustrated hardbacks from his apartment to add to an antique, white bookcase in the dining room. When spring arrives, he adds bulb plants and a variety of perennials to the garden. Our house and garden renovations take place between sex and lines of Victor Hugo's poetry, which David reads one line at a time in perfect French and English. "La vie est une fleur dont l'amour est le miel. Life is a flower, of which love is the honey."

David and I have so much sex the first three months we're together, we both end up with strep throat. The problem is, we just don't sleep much when we're together, even though I take sick days and personal days in an effort to keep up with my degree program and having sex with David. He studies sex as if he's learning a new language. By the fourth month I know I'm addicted to sex. I also know this is really a rebound relationship after my divorce.

"David, I care about you, but maybe I went into this relationship with rose-colored glasses or too many hormones."

I watch him pack his things slowly, leaving his citrus smell in the bedroom armoire, which is the only thing that remains of him. The truth is: Divas have to make the right choices. Once I make a decision, I rarely turn back.

9

Academia

I love a good distraction after an ending. Breaking up with David sends me into a compulsive desire to finish my degree in record time in two subjects that are entirely new to me. At least I got my advisor to get me out of the GRE. Fortunately, I got a sabbatical with pay for a year of study. My life becomes absorbed in studio classes, art history lectures, and Jungian psychology. I'm seeking. I'm striving. I'm in this program with all my heart.

The CU campus in Denver is charming with small older houses that have been converted into offices, meeting rooms, and even a small cafe. Since most of my art classes are three-hour studio classes, I'm on campus Monday through Friday, carrying my portfolio of work along with the type of media needed for a particular class. A large tackle box holds acrylic paints for Charles' studio classes, pastels, and charcoals for life drawing.

In the beginning, I feel out of place in classes full of artists who are my kids' ages. I am in the ultimate world of creative, sometimes complicated, Divas. Before long, I realize I could walk into a studio class in a bikini with lime green hair and no one would even notice.

Coupling my life on campus with my desire to meet new men, starting my business, and becoming wealthy, I am out of control. I feel vulnerable, but I'm not stopping. I remember my favorite artist Berthe Morisot's words about how, when we struggle as artists, we're really struggling with ourselves. Berthe was the only significant female impressionist in the time of Monet,

Degas, Sisley, and Renoir. I channel Berthe's courage and passion every time I paint.

I'd started painting with an impressionistic style but am now becoming more expressionist, studying Jackson Pollock, Robert Motherwell, and his wife, Helen Frankenthaller. I want to look back on this master's program twenty years from now with a smile on my face and a Cosmopolitan in my hand, knowing my life has been a wild adventure even when my mother abused me, my grandfather molested me, and my husband did his best to dampen my Diva spirit.

10

Madonna

"Diane, this is Kiefer. I got your number from your ex-husband. My God, you're free and you are using your maiden name! Morrison is classy, maybe you are related to Jim Morrison. I'm in Denver to visit my son for a few days. Are you still working as a healer for Renew? I would love to schedule a session with you or take you out to a nice restaurant downtown. You can reach me at this number."

Hearing Kiefer's voice takes back to the late eighties when I did Spiritual Direction for Renew, a cutting-edge Catholic healing center run by Father Fred Donson, a Jungian analyst and expert on the Enneagram. Renew was a place of refuge for me during breast cancer. To be honest, I was not a shining example of a devout Catholic, but I did come into this world with a strong intuitive side. My family admired the fact I was praying healing prayer for others while I was healing. I admired the people who created Renew, especially the priest.

"Welcome back, Diane. Finishing chemotherapy in less than a year is quite an accomplishment! May the Lord guide you with your new client today," Father Donson said.

The last time I stopped by Renew, a small red brick house with a black tin roof, everything looked the same as when I worked there. It has an office, three rooms for spiritual direction, and a chapel. The paint colors in the meeting rooms are soothing shades of blue, except for the chapel which is pure white with stencils that looked like fresh violets. The focal point there is still the stained-glass window in shades of dandelion yellow, cobalt blue, and a touch of raspberry. Both the healer and the client are still required to pray in the chapel before a meeting. I remember always looking up at a statue of the Virgin Mary dressed in blue, holding the earth in her hands.

The room was quiet except for the crackling sound of the candle embers hitting the air. I reviewed Kiefer's intake notes one more time before I left the altar.

When I got up, he was standing by the guest book, a tall slim man in black Izod shorts and a navy shirt which accented his deep blue eyes. There was a pack of Marlboro cigarettes sticking out of his shirt pocket along with a small spiral notebook and a bike key. His voice, which sounded like an anchor's voice on the evening news, was strong and seductive. *Jesus, I'm going to be cooped up in a meeting room with this gorgeous man for an hour!* I see an imaginary sign flashing danger inside my head as I feel a rush of hormones.

Our first couple of sessions were mainly about how he became a cocaine dealer. After a couple sessions, I realized he and I are the same personality type. We're extroverts, we love to live out loud, and we're prone to addiction. Kiefer came from a good family. He's very intelligent and seems to have certain beliefs. I would describe him as Catholic with a side-interest in Eastern religion. We had in-depth discussions about many subjects outside of our sessions, usually on the phone at night.

As time went by Kiefer, treated me like some kind of a saint. He still saw me as a Madonna who could save him. The truth was, he also wanted to have sex with me. The more Kiefer and I worked together, the more I struggled with my ethics concerning this client. I ended up going to confession, which I hadn't done since I was a teenager. The attraction between Kiefer and I only got stronger with time. Kiefer's attraction to my Madonna/Whore sides made things complicated for both of us.

Considering the penance a priest gave me in my teens—masturbation = fifty Hail Mary's, looking at magazines unauthorized by the church = twenty-five Our Fathers, etc.—I wondered how much penance I would have to do to make up for having sex with a client?

"Great to hear from you Kiefer. I'm no longer at Renew. Actually, I am working on a master's degree in art and philosophy at Colorado University. You inspired me to make a major change in my life when we spent time together. I have appreciated your yearly birthday messages. It's all about academics for me now. I'm meeting with my philosophy professor at a South American restaurant tonight. It's located at 5366 S. Bannock St. Stop by around seven if you like. You'll probably find me doing Argentine tango."

My art professor, Charles, wants me to meet up with Marta, my philosophy professor, because she is working me too hard and calling me late at night to criticize my research assignments, though I'm not sure if she remembers calling me because she's always in her cups late at night.

"Seduce her a little, Diane, Marta is into women. Do you tango? Marta is a champion! What the hell, do what you need to do. You're only one semester away from your degree. Just be your Diva self; charm her a little and then leave!" Charles laughs.

Marta is giving a handsome South American man a lesson. She's looking at him as if he's something good to eat. Her long, black braid tied with black velvet ribbon moves slowly across her back as she twists her body around her student like a python. Charles could be wrong. It looks like Marta is bisexual.

When another instructor cuts in, Marta loosens up, exposing her long legs accented with textured stockings. She slowly extends her right leg through the slit on her long, black, velvet skirt. After she lowers her black, flouncy, silk blouse over her shoulders, she finishes the tease by moving her black fan in front of her face. Is she flirting with me? Her coal-black eyes focus on me as she finishes her second dance with a different man. I feel she's going to land on me like a fly on flypaper soon.

Marta starts the conversation with, "Diane come to Spain with me after you graduate. It's the perfect place for Divas like us. (This is the first time I dislike being called a Diva because I am not like Marta.) You'll love the cobblestone streets, the spicy cuisine, the deep red sangrias, and the rich hot chocolate. Don't worry about your class with me, you have an A. Your grade is in exchange for giving me permission to include you in my dissertation in the feminine in religion. You're an interesting subject, darling Diva."

Just as Marta starts to pull me onto the dance floor, Kiefer walks in. Thank God.

"My friend just sat down at the bar, Marta. I'll see you in class next week," I say, giving her a reserved hug. The alcohol on her breath is strong. Hopefully she will forget everything she said to me, except the A.

Kiefer looks like a polished business man, dressed in a Mediterranean blue suit. I had never seen him in anything but shorts and casual shirts. Keifer begins, "I'm obsessed with you, Diane. I can't wait until you're ready to be with me. I'm a very successful business owner now. You can have whatever you want. Move to LA with me. Marry me. I have waited a long time to be with you."

"Kiefer, you are a real success story. I know you are sincere about wanting to have a life with me, but I'm not sure I will ever marry again. Getting my master's is taking over my life right now. I have ambitious plans for my future. You are looking for an image of who you think I am, I'm afraid."

Years later, after I become successful, I know I made the right choice the night Kiefer proposed. I did still break a sweat every time Kiefer called, though. He had the bad-boy energy I still crave. Sometimes I think of Kiefer and Julian as two sides of the same coin, but Keifer is charming and upbeat while, above all else, Julian is a goal setter.

11

I'm Just Being Myself

"You look like you could use a drink tonight, Diane," Ryan, the bartender, says. Ryan is a red-headed, Irish mixologist who has a reputation for making the best Cosmopolitan in town, but tonight he's taking care of me with flights of red wine just shipped in from Italy. Ryan cleverly acts as if he's not paying attention to conversations, but he actually listens to every word everyone says.

"Diane, watch out, that's not really a flight; it's three full glasses of wine." Julian laughs as he takes the bar stool next to me.

"I'm not drunk, Julian, I'm just being myself!" Ryan has to turn his head because he's laughing so hard.

The best way I can describe Julian that night is to say he looks prettified in a designer suit and crisp, white shirt with cufflinks, of all things. Julian tends to be either open or reserved. Tonight he's wearing his extrovert mask, so he's more open.

"Hey, Ryan," the woman across from me asks, "Do you have any napkins that say 'I'm not drunk I am just being myself'? Kind of catchy, don't you think?"

"Julian, I haven't heard from you in such a long time. I thought maybe you left your wife, quit your job, and moved to New York to start your own company."

He gives me a look that lets me know he thinks I'm meddling, and I expect him to jokingly ask me what I charge for my services as he often does when I pretend to be his life coach. "Come on, let's get some food into you. We have so much to talk about," he says

My legs are wobbly. I'm having trouble focusing as Julian and I move toward a table. He grabs a menu from the waitress before she has a chance to seat us.

"Hey, chill out, Julian, I'm fine. I'll order my own dinner after I sit down."

I look at the large collection of Tuscan, holy-water fonts on the sunflower-yellow walls. The waitress takes a few minutes to tell me where each font is from: Umbria, Pisa, Sienna. I feel my body melt into the images. "In the name of the Father, the Son, and the Holy Ghost," I say, as I bless myself.

I feel more grounded than drunk now, actually able to feel my face again. While I sip a tall glass of Pellegrino, I listen to Julian make his final choices for dinner. He orders in perfect Italian. Okay, he's pushy, ordering my food as well as his, but that sexy Italian gets me every time. I look at Julian as if he's returning to me from another lifetime, or what some philosophers have called the *eternal return*.

My mind drifts back to when Julian and I first met. It was a chance meeting at a cafe close to downtown Denver. I wore a simple linen dress, a straw hat, and carried a long dangling handmade macramé purse. I guess I looked more like a gypsy Diva but was still stylish for the seventies. I had no idea Julian worked with my ex-husband Anthony at the time.

"You okay, my darling?" Julian asks.

"Sorry, I was thinking about the first time we met. You look amazing, younger than ever, Julian. Seriously, did you check yourself into an ashram to find your true self?"

Julian avoids answering. I could tell he was mulling over the ingredients in the entrees. "Four courses with truffles in each one, even in the dessert," he says, as if he's about to have an amazing sexual experience.

The two of us savor the exquisite meal without excessive talk. We just use words like *transformational, sinful, scrumptious,* and *evocative* to describe the food. I do remember Julian tracing my lips with his index finger as I mention this meal must have been made in Paradise.

We enjoy soufflé di formaggio, insalate, gnocchi, and veal tenderloin, a meal that takes four hours to consume. After we finish, the waitress serves us muddy, black coffee with a selection of biscotti, compliments of the owner. Perhaps I do need to sober up before I drive home. I sit looking at the coffee grounds in the bottom of the cup, just like my grandmother Addie did when she tried to predict the future.

"Diane, I'm divorced. My wife left me for another man. Remember how she spent most of her summers in Italy? She met her new husband in Sienna. Her parents left her an apartment in the center of town. The truth is, I'm single and wealthy now. My ex and I were more like roommates pretending to be lovers. You and I both know I was more of a gigolo than a husband. Maybe we always want what we can't have," he says, with some sadness.

Before I can respond to Julian's surprising news, the waitress brings me a gift-wrapped box with a card from Julian. The package holds a large font with red, blue, and yellow roses around the edges. I'm confused by Julian's vulnerability. Is he telling me he should have been a better husband? Is he gifting me with something I obviously thought meant something to me? Does he want me to see him as a good guy?

Julian tells me he wants me to be a life coach for his company, starting with personality assessments for himself and his employees. He's starting a small advertising company in Denver. "We're past the millennium. The future looks good for a small agency here. I'm flying to New York in two days to shadow a friend of mine who owns an agency in midtown New York. The income you will earn will keep you in all of your favorites: Chanel, Dior, Prada, whatever your heart desires. You'll be the wealthy Diva you've always wanted to be. You've struggled with the restrictions of the public school system. Let that go, and stretch your wings with me!"

I expect him to take me home tonight, now that he's a free man and I'm a free woman. Although I had flirtations with other men when I was married, I was never really unfaithful to Anthony. I had, however, come close to having sex with Julian many times. Is it the possible business connection that created a boundary between us now?

Julian offers to take me to my car because I'm still a little high. "I need to walk," I say, kissing him lightly on the cheek.

It's a starry spring night. The air has a trace of moisture. There are tiny droplets on the leaves of the plants in the manicured gardens in the Cherry Creek North neighborhood. Julian blows me a kiss as he passes in his red Audi convertible, and I feel slightly dazzled by his whole appearance of sudden wealth. Somehow, though, I'm not as attracted to him anymore.

Ryan, the bartender, whispers in my ear before I leave. "This one's a winner, Diane." Yes, it's true: Julian has the polished look of a successful goal-setter. I wonder if his career proposal is mainly the encouragement I need to leave teaching. He's right. I could leave my teaching job, become a life coach, and put my master's degree to work.

In the short time walking to my car, I sense I'm finally ready for a career change. Oh my God, am I ready to leave my adolescent tendencies and leap into adulthood in my fifties? Had I been taking the wrong ferry boat to real life for this long?

While I consider Julian's proposal, I sign up for a series of postgraduate courses with an ex-priest turned professor who calls himself Curly, in spite of the fact he's completely bald.

On the way to north Denver the next morning, I pass a billboard with a beautiful woman driving in her white BMW Convertible with a Louis Vuitton purse on the seat next to her. She's wearing a Dolce & Gabbana scarf that's blowing in the wind. I want a BMW like the one on the billboard someday.

I arrive at the hotel just as Curly, the professor, is helping each attendee in his class choose a nickname. When he comes to me, I tell the group my nickname is Diva. I've always been pretentious and I sometimes blow up when I can't get my own way.

"Diva Diane—I like it. You look fiery with that wild red hair. Are you Irish?" Curly asks as he does an Irish jig. When Curly does an Irish jig, I drift off for a minute. This ex-priest reminds me of another ex-priest who frightened me when I was thirteen years old.

My brothers and I noticed a man dressed in a Roman cassock, sleeping on a bench in a park we always pass on our way to school. Scruffy, as I called him, had chiseled features, an extremely thin body, and dark circles under his eyes. I felt so sorry for him that I couldn't resist moving closer to the bench to offer him my sack lunch. As I got closer, I noticed an open sore on his arm. It looked like he'd tried to carve a skull on his arm. He smelled like fresh blood.

"Good morning, Father, can I help you? Do you need a doctor? Your arm looks sore," I said.

"I'm scared. The streets are full of strangers. I have to hide. I use this cross to protect myself. I'm fighting devils every day."

I come back to the present when Curly asks if anyone in the class has had cancer.

"Why, do I get a prize or free tuition if I had cancer?"

"God bless you, Diva Diane! What would you say has kept you alive? Did you go on a special diet, take more vitamins, or have a spiritual awakening?"

"I did do all those things, but I would say more than anything I became a stronger woman, maybe even pretentious," I say, striking a pose.

After the teachers leave for lunch, Curly asks me to do part of his class the next day.

"Are you offering me a job, Curly? Tell you what: I'll do an art therapy exercise tomorrow. My degree is in art and philosophy. We can talk after my presentation. I hope you pay well."

I begin teaching graduate courses almost overnight. Once I choose to work a second job, I stop pinching pennies to pay my mortgage and start spending money on having a good time. A friend of mine asks how I cope so well. My answer is that I'm letting go of the past. I see the past as an opportunity to learn and grow.

12

Change

My divorce five years ago continues to give me the freedom to become more of a risk-taker than I've ever been. Sure, I can do some life coaching for Julian's company, but I know it would be just another stepping-stone toward owning my own company. Plus, I'm not sure I can travel as much as he would like.

As if Julian can hear me thinking about him, he calls me at midnight from Kennedy Airport with his latest great idea. "Diane, I bought you a gift certificate for the meditation retreat I mentioned the other night. There are two spots left for the session starting this weekend. They will be contacting you tomorrow."

"You're kind of a pushy son of a bitch, Julian, but thanks. I would enjoy some quiet time to think. It will give me the space to take a hard look at my future. Speaking of the future, when are we hooking up? We've been on the edge of having sex for how many years now?" I think about the fact Julian didn't respond to my bold coming on to him. Is he into someone else?

Snow starts to fall as I pack for my week-long meditation retreat. The weather could have given me a good excuse to stay home, sip wine, and gossip with my girlfriends. I scrape the snow off my windshield, noting it's substantial snow for March.

Keeping a Diva like me quiet for more than an hour is quite an accomplishment. What am I thinking? I expect vipassana meditation means closing my eyes, breathing deeply, and repeating a mantra. My overnight bag, a large Louis Vuitton purse, is full of things that will entertain me in case I get bored. In other words, I'm already sabotaging my commitment to silence.

My destination, a retirement home for the Sisters of Peace, is away from the city and rather secluded. I feel more comfortable around city lights. The long entryway is lined with snow-covered blue spruce. I open the window just enough to keep the snow out yet still be able to smell the pine and take in the night sounds. I stop by the side of the road to take a sip of tequila from my flask before I drive up to the convent. I honestly would have been more comfortable spending the night in my car, listening to coyotes and screech owls.

The convent is large, more modern looking than I expected. I imagine there's going to be a moss rock fireplace in a comfortable sitting room where I might have a cup of tea or perhaps a small sherry before the meditation starts. Instead, I'm led to a bland, unappealing conference room where Guru Steve, the leader, is standing at the door to greet me with a tentative handshake. His touch makes my hands feel colder than they felt when I was outside.

"Where's the coffee?" I ask.

"Coffee is a stimulant. There are small juice boxes on the welcoming table," he says.

I pick up a couple of juice boxes, a name tag, and a pen. Everything is marked *Transformation LLC*. The room has poor lighting, discolored tiles from the sixties, and long metallic tables.

There's a cute guy two rows in front of me. I'll keep my eye on him. Maybe we can talk later. Oh wait, this is a silent retreat. Okay, he and I can send hand signals.

The other attendees look stark, sitting in their folding chairs. Are they already in an altered state? I suspect my Diva needs are not going to be met in this room.

A young woman reaches out to me during what Steve calls the connecting part of the meeting, like the sign of peace in a Catholic Mass.

"Namaste," Steve says as he starts sun salutations. It is, of course, nighttime. Afterwards, he lights two tall, plain, white candles and hits the brass gong, signally we are starting meditation. I keep my Chanel purse on my lap because I'm not willing to get my purse stolen in order to become enlightened.

The woman next to me whispers in my ear, "Just breathe. Focus on your breath."

"I want a mantra," I whisper back. My favorite is *Shanti*, which I found out later is a French toast typically used when drinking Champagne.

After the first meditation, Guru Steve addresses me. "Sister, having your purse on your lap is a distraction to us."

Okay, this dude and I are not going to be friends. My designer purse is staying on my lap, or I could just walk out now? Why not? I didn't pay for the conference—Julian picked up the tab. I feel my hand slipping into my purse to touch my flask. Maybe I can manage to get kicked out of this place. I got kicked out of brownies when I was eight years old and almost got kicked out of the Academy.

God, my cell phone is ringing. A stern usher approaches me from the back of the room. I feel his large hands reach for my phone just as Guru

Steve says, "There are no accidents, just a little whisper in your ear that you must follow."

The little whisper in my ear tells me this perfectionist better back off.

"Hey, get your hands off me!" I say to the usher. Rather than make a scene, he backs off. Score one for me!

After the first meditation, we're given juice and crackers with directions to continue meditating in our rooms or do a walking meditation. I'm familiar with the Buddhist monk Thich Nhat Hanh's work on walking meditation, so I go right outside.

The cute guy I saw earlier comes up to me, hands me a candy bar, and continues on the path. I'm going to talk to this guy, whether I get into trouble or not. "Guru Steve is beyond anal-retentive in his approach to helping us become enlightened, don't you think?"

The guy stops, gives me eye contact but keeps his vow of silence. Chemistry without words! Looking at him might keep me quiet for a while. I want more of this!

"Looks like I'll be spending my time outside with you, baby," I wink.

I feel calm, doing a breathing exercise after lights out. I'm shocked I don't feel the need to talk on the phone or drink tequila. An hour later, I come out of what feels like a trance. My body is limp as I slip further under the disgusting old blanket on my bed.

Since I never have breakfast before nine, I don't have time to dress for breakfast at seven. What the hell, my designer, cream, satin bathrobe will have to do.

I see a nun standing next to an old-fashioned black piano, looking like a guard outside a prison cell. Her eagle eyes are directed right at me as she shakes a chastising finger. I guess she's not into bedroom attire. I just shrug my shoulders as her face turns beet red. No sense of humor, I guess. She and Sister Cecilia, my middle school principal, would get along well.

The white-walled dining room smells stuffy. The dull fluorescent lighting makes the vegetarian buffet look gray and unappealing. A younger, friendlier nun leaves her station to help me with the dark brown, dirty food tray I'm holding. She starts talking to me as I move my small scarf to the side to expose my name tag which reads *SILENCE,* but she continues to talk. I'm really conflicted now. Should I break my vow of silence, risking going to hell for ignoring a nun? I compromise by letting her choose my food. Instead of speaking, I give her hand signals: thumbs up, hang loose, whatever works.

I make it back to another utilitarian, aluminum picnic table which has an eating doctrine on a small stand: Observe mindful eating by taking slow bites, paying attention to your breathing, and avoid eye contact with anyone. Eating is a form of meditation. Take the prayer book sister hands you when you finish eating. Only read our material during your stay. —Guru Steve

The cute guy gives me forbidden eye contact as he leaves the dining room. So sexy.

There's a fresh bouquet of yellow tulips in a glass vase on my desk when I return to my room. My cell phone rings, probably Julian letting me know he sent the flowers.

It's as if the Guru can smell my phone. Since we have to leave our bedroom doors open, he walks right in and points to my phone. *No, no, no,* I feel him say without speaking. I mouth back, "Jerk, jerk, jerk!"

Not typically an anxious person, I feel myself starting to hyperventilate a little because I haven't spoken for almost twenty-four hours. I'm rarely introverted, but I did like hanging out in the zone last night, so I'm not leaving yet. Besides, I'm expected to be in the meditation room in five minutes.

When I enter the room, Guru Steve gives me a chastising look as if I'm not perfect enough to enter the room. I give him the finger but I guess he is too into himself to see the gesture. The usher is back. I wonder if he saw what I just did? Where are those nuns that were here earlier today? I could use a good Hail Mary right now, but there's not a single nun on site.

There are small, brass bowls filled with burning sage in every corner of the meditation room. I walk around the room, taking in the smell. Maybe sage is supposed to ward off evil spirits. Attendees who are assisting Steve begin to chant. Every now and then, the Buddha and Mother Mary are mentioned. Okay, I know Mary—I grew up saying the Rosary. The room is actually in the Virgin's favorite shade of blue, but it's the statue of the Buddha, not the Virgin, that finally draws me into silence. I don't know the Buddha that well, but I know to sit cross-legged on one of the bright-colored, silk pillows, most likely made in India.

Since I have been told not to block thoughts while meditating, I let a memory of my grandmother Tilly pass.

I see Tilly, my father's mother, sitting in a red chair in her small garden in Brooklyn. I can almost smell the turned earth. I felt the dry seeds sifting through my fingers as Tilly told me there is power in a seed. Together we created a colorful map of where all the flowers will grow. Time passed slowly in Tilly's garden.

She fixed tiny sandwiches, like her mother used to make for her. The sandwiches were cut into different shapes. Tilly laughed at the screeching crows who hovered around the crusts of bread left from the cookie cutters. Tilly and I dressed up when we worked in the garden. She was in brown slacks and a blue blazer. I was wearing a bright orange and white pinafore. I never thought about Tilly being a Diva, but I see now she does have a classy sense of style.

When I returned to Tilly's garden later in the summer, the dahlias were in full bloom. Some were as tall as me. The neighbor's German shepherd jumped our fence and landed on my favorite flowers. I felt his slimy tongue lick off my face cream. Tilly took pictures of me laughing, in spite of the dahlias being torn up.

The next day, Tilly took me to New York City to shop. The sales ladies at B. Altman called me Shirley Temple because of my curly hair. I tried on two polka-dot dresses, white cotton skirts with sleeveless blouses, pink cotton shorts, and a red bathing suit. The manager of the store watched me dance around in the yellow polka-dot dress. I acted just like I did when I performed for the Harpers in Jersey City. I must have been nine when the store manager approached Tilly about me modeling for B. Altman, which I knew would never happen because anything connected with the Morrison's was treated with scrutiny.

"Your granddaughter could model for us. She's quite the Diva. Do you mind if our photographer takes a few shots of her?" the manager asked.

Damn, I'm not getting anywhere with meditating today. My Type 7 personality is known as *monkey mind*, a mind that's always on.

When I step outside, I see a tall Asian man walking on a different path leading to the back of the convent. He motions to me to share a bench with him by a cage of love birds. When his eyes close, I close mine. I listen to the sound of snow melting as I begin to match his breathing. I'm finally free of my thoughts.

Guru Steve comes outside to call me in for today's closing ceremony, which is really all about asking for donations. After the money is in the collection basket, Guru Steve signals that the vow of silence has ended.

"Aren't you glad now you didn't take my purse away, Guru Steve?" I say, heading out the convent door.

13

Beautiful Image

When the retreat is over, I drive to Boulder to spend the rest of my spring break with my professor and mentor Charles. It takes me awhile to get there from the convent because I've forgotten how to be in a hurry and I like that. Everything I pass on the road to Boulder looks exaggerated. The colors of the trees are more vibrant. The sky is bluer. It's like I'm on drugs, but I haven't taken anything except meditation.

Charles is in a robe when I arrive, which means he has been nude in the garden. "The party is here!" Charles says, as if I'm ready to drink and raise hell. Well, I have been at a silent retreat for a few days so I accept a cup of his famous Irish coffee as I beg off talking about being in a convent pretending I'm trying to find my authentic self. "Long story," I say about the retreat. "Great studio, Charles. Much bigger than the one you had in Santa Fe."

I kiss him, catching the tickle of his Chantilly-covered beard on my face.

The studio is painted in a shade of yellow that looks like lemon juice surrounded by white enamel molding. Nude paintings hang on the thick walls, accented by the ceiling lights. Charles has three easels set up in the main room. One has a partially finished landscape, the other looks like his cottage in Santa Fe, and the third has a canvas that only reveals the back of the piece.

"Congratulations, Diane! You have let go of many of your attachments from the past: a dead marriage, financial dependence, and probably boredom. It sounds as if new career opportunities are in your path. The master's degree is going to help you, my precocious Diva!"

"You told me to get out of my marriage when I took your writing workshop in Santa Fe. *Dead* and *destruction* were the descriptors you used to describe my thirty-year marriage to Anthony. I lost my right breast soon after the trip."

We move to a small sitting room next to the studio. The sitting room is both vibrant and cozy, which is hard to achieve from a design sense. A clear crystal vase of raspberry-colored flowers is reflected in a large mirror hung on a turquoise wall.

Charles jumps out of his overstuffed, yellow, velvet chair when I tell him I'm walking away from my secure teaching career of twenty-some years. He's so excited that his robe falls to the floor, leaving him naked in the middle of the room. Well, it's not like I haven't seen him without clothes before.

"Synchronicity!" Charles says as he directs me back into the studio. I watch him grab a pencil to personalize the back of the painting on one of his easels. *To Artemis, the goddess of the hunt and the moon. You are the strongest woman I know. Love, Charles.*

My mind is racing because we talked about Artemis in one of Charles's art history classes. The goddess Artemis cut off her right breast to increase her ability to hunt with a bow and arrow.

Charles reveals he snapped a couple of photos of me at Wave the first time I took a writing class with him in Sante Fe. "I can still hear you snoring on a bench next to the soaking pool when I photographed you. The Diva in you came out so easily in your cheeky pose," he laughs.

I really want to take a photo of him showing me what I expect is a nude of me, but I'm too overwhelmed by the painting to do anything but cry. "Damn, Charles, you created the last image of my right breast."

Charles holds me against his chest for a long time. His loving warmth fills me as he encourages me to cry, but of course I resist because I don't grieve easily. Charles' gardener comes through the studio door, setting me free from my feelings for a minute.

When Charles returns from his garden, he asks how my love life is going. He laughs when I tell him the most adventurous men are from Boulder, some of them twenty-five years younger than me.

"You have the energy of a much younger woman, so why not younger men?" he asks.

Monet, Charles' French bulldog, barks the minute he sees Charles take out his leash. After we finish our walk through downtown Boulder, Charles hands me a check for two pieces of art he sold from my thesis show at CU.

"Why don't you use this money to take a trip to Nice before you start your new career? You would be doing me a favor because I'm in a gallery in old Nice. I'm thinking of showing more of my work in France and possibly moving to Nice eventually."

Before I leave for Denver that day, Charles and I take a hike up Boulder Canyon. After I tell him about Julian's offer to have me be a life coach for his company, Charles gives me a piece of his mind. "Listen, Julian has been in and out of your life for many years. Julian is a classic gigolo, and I suspect that he's leading you on again. He'll use your expertise and then move on as usual. Why don't we call my lawyer after lunch to discuss setting up a corporation for you. He's a fan of your work. Think of your experiences with teaching graduate courses now as part of your journey toward having your own consulting company."

As the two of us and Monet go back into the oak forest to gather mountain blueberries, Charles pulls a few flat, yellow flowers that grow between the rocks. He claims they increase testosterone, and I give him a thumbs up and mention Renaissance Man's high level of testosterone. Charles laughs so hard he sends a flock of mountain jays out of an oak tree.

When we return home, Charles cooks a light pasta for lunch. He makes the meal into a contest, using sensual words to describe food.

"It's getting steamy in here," I say as I trace shapes on the moist kitchen window.

I pour two glasses of Chianti to go with the spicy vegetarian pasta. My hand starts to tremble as Charles tells me my latest writing from the silent retreat is honest. Hook the reader with more narrative, use your sensual words, go slow like you do when you mix a cocktail, he says. Writing is more like making a Cosmopolitan than pouring tequila into a shot glass.

I did a solo Latin dance for Charles as a thank you after lunch. He did quick sketches of me in different dance positions, which I received several years later at his memorial. Charles always treated me like a daughter even though he was only a few years older than me.

14

Play Before Work

My short, white dress with a string of Chanel pearls gets me some attention on the Rue de Republique as I walk to the Negresco Hotel. One man in particular asks, "Tu veux sortir avec moi, Diva?" *Do you want to go out with me, Diva?*

Apparently Diva is the same in French and in English. I give the French man a cheeky smile and a polite, "Non, merci."

The bar at the hotel smells like old booze and cigarette butts. There are flies all over the dish of lemons and limes. Not a good night to order a gin and tonic, I decide. I can deal with the flies because the bar has a nice flair, and you can't beat the sound of waves combined with music.

"Bonsoir Monsieur, I'll have a Kir Royale. By the way, who's the singer?"

"She's Lara, a pop singer who's becoming popular in southern France. I wish she was my sister. I love her so much! I can sell you one of her CDs. Her newest one is *Diva*," he says.

I watch a young girl dressed in blue and white beach clothes dancing to Lara on the other side of the bar. Her beautiful, raven hair moves from side to side, exposing her childlike features now and then. She starts to sing, "Tu m'oublieras"—*you will not forget me*—as if she means every word.

"You're from New York City, am I right?" asks the bartender, showing his white foam mustache which he immediately wipes on his black and white apron.

"Why?" I ask. "Do I have city soot on my face?"

Before he can answer me, the girl I've been watching asks him for a set-up of Absinthe and signals to a tall, thin ginger she calls Juliette. The two women begin talking about Galerie Eve, the gallery where Charles is showing some of his work. It only takes me a few minutes to decide these two sultry beauties are more than business acquaintances. They can't stop making out at the bar. I ask Juliette the name of her perfume which is filling the bar with its pungent scent.

"Any perfumery in Nice can mix this one for you, Madame. Just ask for N'Aimez que Moi," Juliette says, in a thick New York accent. The two of us compare the art scene in New York and Nice until her girlfriend looks as if she's going to have a temper tantrum.

The next morning, Yann, the gallery owner, greets me with a compliment as I enter Galerie Eve. "I'm shocked Charles hasn't painted you, Diane. I'll have to speak to him," he says, kissing me on both cheeks.

I shiver as I look around Galerie Eve because it's the type of gallery I would love to open someday. Yann tells me that the small space in the heart of old town Nice is dedicated to art from the nineteenth to twenty-first centuries. Yann knew the family who owned the space—which had been owned by the same family for seventy-five years. He has maintained the original charm and kept some of the pieces that came with the purchase. Yann is also adding touches of modern paintings to the walls. Yann favors large paintings by local pop artists: pieces similar to work that emerged in the early nineties in the US. When he shows me his private collection of Mapplethorpe's photographs, he begins to cry.

Charles will be represented well by Yann, a sensitive owner who has the best *galerie* in the middle of Nice. Its view of the ocean and contemporary flair draw serious collectors from all over the world. I admire Yann's black leather journal, which he uses to record my remarks about the various collections. The last collection is sculpture in an outside garden. Something like Rodan's work by a young artist who lives close to the gallery.

There's something dangerous and delicious about the freedom I feel in the Cote d'Azur. I've walked here more than anywhere else. It's the sea air and the beautiful surroundings of blue and white chairs and umbrellas that catch my eye on the beach that's rocky until it reaches the water.

When Yann invites me to dinner that evening, I can't resist because this Frenchman is very charming. "Bring a bathing suit if you want to enjoy the pool before dinner, of course. Nude bathing is fine in Nice, as you must know. Here's a key to the pool if you arrive before me."

I feel comfortable about swimming nude, but I wonder if Yann will notice the scars on my breasts. I'm just not in the mood to go into the whole breast cancer story tonight. Since he doesn't know I had cancer in the eighties, I don't want him to know now. He might start feeling sorry for me. If he touches my breasts, he will conclude I have implants purely for cosmetic reasons.

Yann doesn't notice my scars. Apparently, I'm the only one who is concerned about my breasts, as Dora has told me many times. As I dry off with a large blue and white beach towel, Yann throws a large steak on the grill. I love the sound of crackling meat.

Before I grab my dress from the changing room, I watch the way this French man sniffs the wine before he pours with a sense of gravitas. He tells me wine is more precious than gold. The glasses he uses are wide, allowing the richness of the wine to fill the sea air. The sound he makes as he takes his first sip causes me to put him on my list of possible yummy lovers.

"Diane, I want to take you to a tasting at Châteauneuf-du-Pape someday. This Burgundy is one of theirs. Magnificent, don't you think? I was a wine merchant for many years while I practiced law, but the *galerie* absorbs all of my passion now. You know, you really should live in France, darling. This country is the place for Divas."

The next morning is full of the sound of sheep bells in the distance and black crows landing on the red roof above my room. I wash the night off my face before I have a cafe creme with Yann.

I leave him with a sincere promise I will return. It's hard to leave him to catch the TGV at Gare de Nice, but he understands my new company launches a month after I return to Denver.

When I see Juliette board the train, I watch her ponder the seating. She leaves her luggage on a shelf and heads to the dining car. I'm tempted to join her, but I take out my half-bottle of rosé and a petite sandwich I picked up at the *gare*.

Juliette returns with a large bottle of rosé, which she uses to refill my wine glass and hers after she takes the last seat on the train next to me. I must admit the chemistry between Juliette and Chloe at the Negresco Bar was stimulating. If I ever want to try being with a woman, Juliette would be one to consider. Before she leaves the train in Avignon, Juliette invites me to visit her in NYC.

"We'll see," I say, which really means *no*.

The best thing about international flights out of Paris is the free alcohol, good food, and plenty of pampering. As soon as I have my fill of vodka and then red wine with dinner, I adjust my earphones to block out noise as I plan to zone out during the long night flight.

"Are you alright, madame? You've been singing in your sleep."

"French or English?" I ask as she offers me coffee.

"Definitely French, madame."

"Mais bien sur!

15

Success Outside the Box

I'm done living in America's gray-scale boring boxes. I'm done being a conventional housewife. I can't go to work for someone else's corporation. I have to have my own company!

Once Diane Morrison Consulting, a training company for teachers, becomes a reality, I don't have time to dwell on the past. It's all forward-thinking for me now. No one better try to put the brakes on me. I feel the power of being a woman who has known she wanted to be an entrepreneur all of her adult life. I'm passionate, curious, and my brain is always on. I often lay awake thinking about courses I want to develop and how I will present myself to an audience.

Thank God I bought new clothes in Nice a couple of months ago: black pencil skirts with blazers accented with business pumps, colorful scarves, and of course, bright red lipstick. I'm dripping with power colors the first time I enter the hotel as Professor Diane Morrison.

My first day as an entrepreneur reminds me of what I no longer have to deal with: administrator evaluations, difficult parents, children to face. Every day, millions of people earn their keep in boring office spaces or crowded classrooms. Owning my own company will give me the freedom I crave. I'm living outside the box, just waiting to spend money on travel, eating in fine restaurants, and filling my walls with beautiful paintings!

I walk into the conference room feeling like a confident Diva. The hotel manager treats me as if I'm someone important as she helps me set up for the day. The room is pleasant, as far as conference rooms go. Big windows allow for plenty of natural light, round tables encourage teachers to connect with each other in a manner that rarely happens during a typical work day. Most teachers rarely leave their classrooms because they're too busy dealing with problems, making lesson plans, and grading papers. Teachers deserve to be in a nice learning environment. My plan is to give teachers cutting edge material in an environment that feels like a getaway weekend.

For what feels like a long agonizing minute, I survey the room of teachers, meeting everyone's gaze with a warm smile. After an exquisitely-timed pause, I yell out, "Are you ready to change your life?"

The audience of forty teachers looks exhausted from their third week back in school after summer vacation. I'd better be on my game today. I'm facing a bar crowd; my audience looks hungover. I'm determined to win them over.

Once again, I burble, "Are you ready to change your life? Can you believe that you're sitting in this beautiful hotel, ready to take the most amazing class you've ever taken?"

I feel like I'm Tony Roman, a motivational speaker, as I watch the entire group of teachers stand up and yell back, "Yes!" I have the audience in the palm of my hand. The last thing I want is to offer a boring in-service. I had to sit through enough of them when I was teaching kids.

Very few teachers know anything about my subject, the Enneagram. I'm the only professor in Colorado who is offering graduate credit for what I believe is the most powerful personality study available. The Enneagram was passed down to communities over two-thousand years ago in storytelling form, and I am a storyteller today. The room is as full of as much energy as the concert I attended at Red Rocks Amphitheater last summer. My God, these teachers look so different now than when they first entered the conference room. Not one looks apathetic anymore. I feel like I've had five cups of coffee because the teachers are energizing me.

The football coach who told me he was here just to get the credit is engaged in what I have to say. When I get to his personality type, *the Boss*, he tells everyone in the room he doesn't get mad, he gets even. The audience laughs when I jokingly tell him he has an A.

"Little lady," the coach says, "you're fun. I'd like to buy you a beer after class. You're my kind of professor."

The anxious woman in the back has finally stopped interrupting me with questions. She knows I'm making sure she's safe and secure with me. Oh, and the cowboy dressed in full garb, including spurs, is fully into finding out more about his personality type. Teachers are a good audience. They get it; they speak for a living. My desire to interact with everyone in the audience is like an endless itch. I can't stop myself. It's never too late to find your perfect niche, and now I realize that speaking is mine.

On my way home from the hotel, I open the windows, filling the car with fall smells. My mind is clear, my heart is full. If I could dance in the middle of the street, I would, but I'll save that until tonight.

As soon as I unload my materials, I head into the French garden with a glass of wine and a small dish of potato chips: a typical French happy hour, or as they say, happy *hours*. Brilliant! I prefer the thought of more than one hour of drinking.

I begin my company at the end of September, 1999, and by December I'm doing well enough to expand by hiring three professors to teach classes.

By the following June, I stop teaching classes for Curly and never actually did life coaching for Julian's company. I started the company at my kitchen table. Now I have made enough money to create a small office space, which opens to a courtyard, in my home.

As time passes, I realize Dora was accurate in her predictions about my success because, within a year, we are the top teacher training company in Denver. When my daughter, Michelle, becomes an officer of the corporation, she frees up more time for me to do more research on the brain, goal setting, emotional intelligence, and more. Michelle is left-brained and I'm right-brained; together we have a perfect brain, with each of us playing to our strengths.

Soon after I become the top consulting company in Denver, I start getting hate mail from my old boss, Curly. I have to contact my lawyer because things get bad. Curly had actually started showing up at my house, verbally abusing me for ruining his business. I loved Curly like a father. He reminded me of my stepfather Sam, but in the end he is not like the Sam I remember.

I will never forget when Sam came into my life. I was living in Jersey City the night I met him. I remember staring at the bottom of the wooden stairs, waiting for Sam to walk up into the apartment. Will he think we're poor? The walls by the stairs were covered with dull paint, the lights were dim, and the steps were filthy, but when I saw Sam running up the stairs carrying homemade ice cream, I felt my heart melt like the ice cream.

I guess I thought Curly intended to change my professional life, the way Sam changed my personal life. I became well known in the academic world faster than I could have ever imagined. The truth is, I could no longer risk being associated with an unprofessional company like Curly's. My friend Bruce, who is now one of my most popular professors, teases me about having been a petite redhead who used to teach kindergarten and is now kicking ass in the business world. The bigger I get, the more of a Diva I become. Female teachers often admit they take my classes just to see what I'm wearing. They call me Diva and the Guru Professor. The guru connection doesn't fit me, but I do become more of a Diva the more successful I become.

16

The Return

My party-girl side needs attention. Bruce is teaching this weekend. I'll stop by the hotel to remind the teachers about how important it is to sign up for more classes. "Get the credit and the raise!"

Instead of calling a girlfriend to sit at a bar with me tonight, I leave my business clothes in the closet, put on a short black dress and purple heels, and carry my matching purple purse.

Ryan puts out a nice setup of mixed nuts, breadsticks, olive oil, and a small glass of Pellegrino. After two of Ryan's signature Cosmopolitans, I order a glass of house white wine and a small dish of pasta with pesto. It's a Friday night, and even though the bar is full, Ryan and I play our usual game of "who's my type of guy?" When he points out a tall, fair redhead, I make it clear that he's definitely off his game tonight.

"What about that Julian you were with a few months ago?" he asks.

"Julian has been in and out of my life for so many years, Ryan. He's annoyed with me because I didn't take his offer to be a life coach for his company. I have my own company now."

Ryan brings me a piece of Tiramisu and an espresso—a celebration for me—and hands me the name of a friend of his, a successful realtor. "Check this guy out, call him, or give me your card and he'll call you."

It's Monday morning, time to chill at Stella's Coffee House. As soon as I sit down by the fountain in the back, I feel relaxed. The *Westword* newspaper sitting next to me on the table is open to the romance ads. *Successful artist looking for a creative, dynamic woman who is a soul-searcher.*

When I call the number, the message says, "My name is Glassman, not bad for a glass artist. Leave me a message."

"I'm Diane, not bad for a goddess. God, I'm being a smart ass, sorry. Feel free to call me."

It's a cool fall night when I see my date looking inside the cafe. When he turns around, I almost jump out of my skin.

"Oh my God, Alex, is that you? I wondered if I would ever see you again after I stopped taking life drawing classes. Remember how embarrassed I was when you came to my table to complement my black boots?"

"Diane, it's good to see you again. I do remember talking to you in life drawing class. Do you remember looking at the ceiling the whole time we talked? I guess you still saw me naked, even though I was wearing a robe. By the way, didn't you tell me your son got one of your pastel drawings of me?"

We talk for hours, catching up on his time on a vineyard and my time setting up my own company. Alex's stories about becoming vegan in boar country in southern France took me back to my visit to Nice. Alex loved working in the vineyard, in the botanical gardens, and in the cork museum on the grounds.

"Wine is seductive. I would love to have my own vineyard, but it's back to my stained-glass studio for me. I'm also making jewelry and painting. The owner of the vineyard sent me home with two cases of wine. Would you like to come to my apartment for dinner this week?"

Denver is hit with a major blizzard in the middle of September, forcing me to postpone my visit to Alex's apartment. The tree branches are bending over from the weight of heavy snow in my front and back yards. I can't get out of either of my doors to shake the snow off the trees.

My God, Alex is outside shoveling snow off my front porch. He waves to me and points to the bag of groceries which he puts inside right away.

"Helping a pampered Diva are you, Alex?" He laughs when I try to start a fire in the old fireplace in the living room. Fortunately, Renaissance Man left a nice pile of wood in the backyard before he moved out. It turns out to be a cozy day. We fix dinner together, drink wine, and play Scrabble before he returns to his apartment for the night.

Three days later, Alex invites me for dinner. His apartment is small: a kitchen, a bedroom, and a small sitting room. The walls in the living room are covered with unframed watercolor paintings he did on the vineyard last summer. My favorite painting is of a single asparagus, similar to the Manet I saw at the Musée d'Orsay in Paris more than a year ago.

Alex serves a simple yet elegant meal. The salad and the cooked vegetables come from his garden in the back of the apartment. The salmon is prepared with goat cheese and cilantro. The wine is from the vineyard in Provence. "The thing about wine, Diane, is if I open this bottle today it would taste different than if I opened it yesterday. Wine is alive!" Alex says, with a twinkle in his eye.

After dinner, he tells me he was raised an Orthodox Jew, but his apartment is full of pictures of different gurus. I am confused by his interest in me, a materialistic Diva. Alex is clearly a minimalist. Maybe introverts like him are drawn to extroverts like me. What is it with these introverts? Do they have repressed sexuality? When we have sex, he explodes like a volcano. I sense a freedom in Alex I haven't experienced in other men. He knows who he is and I suspect he will not try to control me like other men have.

Alex moves into the Blue Room on a sunny day in early November, two months after we met. He comes in with four boxes of clothes, a couple of small paintings, some of his stained glass, and his last case of French wine. The transition from single life to coupling is surprisingly easy for us. We're close, but we each like our own space. Alex makes it clear he wants to support my vision of success. He graciously takes over some of the household chores while I run my consulting company, a perfect arrangement for a Diva. My mind is swirling with the amount of freedom I have in this relationship.

After several months of living together, Alex asks if I would consider getting married. I suggest a session with Dora.

Two days later we're in the car headed for Dora's office in downtown Boulder. We arrive on time, but no one is there to greet us. I lead Alex through the beaded curtain to get to the sitting room. Dora's collection of cream-colored candles are lit and the silver tea service is set up as usual. Dora enters the room, looking professional in her light gray suit and lavender silk blouse as if she's right on time.

"Diane, you mentioned you two have been living together for six months. How is that going?"

Before we have a chance to answer, Dora closes her eyes. "Oh boy, she's going into one of her trances," I whisper in Alex's ear.

"I'm getting past life information about both of you. Alex, you knew Diane as a goddess in your last life. You were one of her devotees. You worshipped her, so to speak."

Good thing Jim, Dora's assistant, enters the room with both of our astrology charts. Alex looks like he's ready to run out of the room as fast as he can after hearing the goddess statement.

"Diane and Alex, you have the same degree of Cancer in your rising signs," Dora says.

I don't know what the hell she's talking about, but Alex nods his head in agreement. Alex knows astrology. I can add this information to the list of things I didn't know about the man I'm thinking of marrying. For instance, Alex joined the Peace Corps to avoid the draft, he lived in India for a while, and he was a caretaker for an aging guru in Boston.

"Your charts indicate you are quite compatible, as far as I can tell. Both of you love your home space. Diane, you like traveling more than Alex does, but he will always join you. I predicted your success the first time we met, Diane. You two are going to have enough money to do whatever you want."

After the three of us enjoy a cup of Earl Grey tea, Dora blesses us with her words of wisdom. "If you find yourselves asking a question about how you are living your lives together, consider three golden rules: Are you being good to yourselves as individuals? Are you being good to each other as a couple? Are you aware life is a relationship with everything in the universe? Let me know if you would like me to marry you. Namaste."

I know I'm better at understanding men now than when I married Anthony, but the truth is, I broke up with most of the men I thought I loved. Dora thinks I have a hard time trusting men because Pop sexually abused me at a young age.

"There's something I need to tell you, Alex. I've dealt with PTSD most of my life because my grandfather sexually abused me. My mother never confronted him. She felt we should be grateful he gave us a roof over our heads after my father was killed."

"I have friends who have PTSD from serving in Viet Nam. Take your time getting help. I understand why making a long-term commitment with another man after being married for thirty years would be hard," he says, with compassion in his eyes.

Later that night we have wine in the Blue Room. I look at Alex. He looks at me. We have our differences, but we think back on the good times we had this year. My main concerns about Alex are that he tends to check-out in order to spend time on the computer, and when he's upset he gets loud and repeats himself. I wasn't familiar with the word Asperger's at the time. I decided being a creative person and an observer personality were in line with Alex's tendencies.

Later that night, Alex and I sit quietly in the Blue Room. We look at our large oil painting of a man and woman facing each other. "That's us, the couple in the painting. We connect very well at an intellectual level. We have our differences, but doesn't every couple?" Alex asks.

The phone rings before I can answer Alex's question.

"Alex, my friend Julian wants me to visit him for a long weekend in New York, all expenses paid. He probably has another business proposition for me."

"Sure, it might be good for us to have a little time apart," he says.

Julian has an apartment on the upper east side. Guessing I would prefer separate space, he got me a suite in my favorite hotel close to Central Park and the Metropolitan Museum.

The New York skyline is pure glitter from the hotel's rooftop garden. I notice the red and white tip of an Italian flag flying from an apartment building close to the hotel. Oh, my God it must be close to Columbus Day. New York is one of the few cities in the US that still honors the controversial explorer.

I remember marching in the Columbus Day Parade every year I was at the Academy because all the nuns, including the lovely Mother Barbara, were Italian. Of course I felt humiliated marching in my ugly, burgundy uniform with my polished saddle shoes. The parade always started on 44th Street and 5th Avenue. We followed the police band, followed by an entourage of more police on white motorcycles. Mother Barbara arranged to have a band from the all-boys Academy close to our Academy march in front of us. We wore tall hats covered with black fur and we twirled our ribbon-tied batons. Most of my classmates were Italian. I often wondered just how many of my classmate's fathers were in the Mafia.

My lips begin to quiver when Julian comes toward me with a bouquet of blood-red chrysanthemums, a bottle of Champagne, and two Tiffany wine glasses. "Diva," he says as he hands me a large Dolce & Gabbana box. He laughs at my shaky hands trying to untie the bright colored bow.

"Here darling, let me help you. A Diva needs a crown," he says.

I adjust the crown while Julian pours the Champagne as a rather taciturn group of three French waiters walk past us with small, gold plates of appetizers and beautiful stark-white linen napkins. One waiter serves foie gras, the other serves mussels in cream sauce, and the third finishes with Swiss chard ravioli. We watch a second group of waiters set up tables with French blue linens and white asters in navy blue vases.

"My God, Julian you always feed me the most elegant food. You should write for a food and travel magazine. Did you rent the rooftop just for us?"

"Yes, I did rent the rooftop, and actually, I do send recipes to *Bon Appetit*, Diane," Julian says with pride.

The head waiter announces our second course. "Madame and monsieur, we have here fresh sea bass with potato puree, a selection of root vegetables with a lemon butter glaze, and small purple potatoes from the island of Molokai fried in Irish butter."

Julian pours our second wine, a Cote de Rhone from Châteauneuf-du-Pape. "Stay with me," he says, as he kisses my neck.

A young jazz singer sets up a microphone in front of a magnificent fall sunset. She sounds like Sade, one of my favorite Divas. I know it isn't coincidental that her first song is "Come Away With Me."

The waiter notices Julian and I dancing so close he leaves the rooftop, I suppose, to let the chef know we are not ready for dessert, at least not the edible kind.

I hear Julian say, "Please serve the toasted stracciatella ice cream, a bottle of chestnut liqueur, and espresso in Madame's suite in thirty minutes."

There are so many things Julian still doesn't know about me and probably never will. I suspect the magnetic pull between us over the years would be judged by some people. After dessert is served, we let the ice cream melt and the espresso grow cold. I wonder if fate will finally set us free.

I take a glass of chestnut liquor out on the balcony. Julian is gone when I return.

When I return to Denver, I realize Alex and I have our good memories together. I decide to move forward with an almost blind trust. I put my concerns aside when Alex asks me to marry him.

Dora calls to find out about my trip to New York.

"How was the gigolo? Did he tempt you again?" she laughs her typical spiky laugh.

"What happens on the upper east side, stays on the upper east side. Bad boys like Julian are a lot of fun, but I know they're not good for a functional relationship. I know I get addicted to the roller coaster. I'll slowly detox from the thrills I get from Julian and learn to get my thrills elsewhere."

"It's tough because Julian is a Hustler, he's your Diva counterpart. Maybe he even makes you a bit of a Hustler. It's okay to call women Hustlers now."

Nine months after visiting Julian in New York, Alex and I are making tentative wedding plans. It turns out Alex would prefer a casual wedding in the backyard. After the ceremony, he would like our guests to be able to create art and play games in our yard. According to my youngest brother, Pat, I want something more like a Diva's dream prom and Alex wants a kind of a hippy art fest. We compromise by having a casual rehearsal dinner in the backyard and the wedding in a French restaurant.

Alex chooses a colorful linen suit and I opt for a pink dress similar to my mother's wedding dress. Two packages arrive from Veronica the same day that Alex and I are looking at restaurants for our reception. The packages contain a torn, pink dress, a string of pearls, and a journal. I can almost crawl inside my mother's head as I read her first journal entry.

June 10, 1940

I'll be sitting under a pink hairdryer at Le Belle Salon today. Pink is my color. No need to wear a white wedding dress. The ladies at the salon will help me get into my pink and white frock I made myself.

June 11, 1940

There was a light morning breeze in the air as I stepped outside the salon to catch my breath. Looking back through the large picture window, I realized the next time I have my hair done I will be a married woman. After I shared a glass of Champagne with the hairdressers, I felt elegant. Yet knew I was moving toward something disobedient, even sinful. I was choosing a husband who was not Catholic, but my body shivered because my lover and I were eloping against our parents' wishes.

I stepped out of the cab, left foot forward. The echo of the bottom of my shoe scraped the gravel as the taxi driver remarked I had sureness in my step.

Robert was standing in his summer army uniform, khaki jacket with brass buttons, white shirt, khaki trousers, brimmed hat, and black army shoes. I ran across the grass to meet him. My right foot turned as I went down on the cement walkway. Is this a bad omen, I wondered? My pink dress was torn in three places and blood dripped from my knees, staining part of my dress. The photographer took a few shots of us before we left for the Hudson County Courthouse. He claimed he could take out the scrapes on my face later. I put my hand over the worst of them.

The interior of the courthouse was dull with mostly Fuzzy Wuzzy brown paint. The stained glass in the rotunda at the entrance allows light to flood the room. The Justice of the Peace cocked his head to the left, probably wondering why my face was scraped and my dress was torn. He proceeded with simple words. The wedding ceremony was just a formality as a strong sexual bond had already been established between Robert and me.

I can't believe my mother may have actually been knocked up before she got married. Maybe this is why she was hard on me about getting pregnant in my teens. Was it all just her own projection?

Now here's the question of the day: did I really have a twin brother or was Veronica covering her ass because she was pregnant on her wedding day? Is the story she told me about her miscarriage and my being born a month before my due date true? Yet, there was the phone call I got from my Aunt Marjorie a couple of years ago. Marjorie said when Veronica was four months pregnant, she fell down a flight of stairs which resulted in a miscarriage. Then the doctor heard a second heartbeat: mine.

What is the pale, flickering screen of a vaguely defined figure we each perceive as a parent? Memories of a parent can be strong in one moment and vague in the next. I'm seeing Veronica in myself when Alex and I talk about the wedding. It is easier to see her positive traits now.

17

The Pink Wedding Dress

I've had enough of being in my mother's head. After reading Veronica's diary, I hope to find a designer who can make a dress that will have pieces of Veronica's wedding dress with a nineties style and Chanel flair. In fact, an artist friend of mine is designing and sewing dresses for a few clients. I'll start with her.

While I admire my mother's wedding dress from the mid-forties, I need a modern look to satisfy my Diva style. My friend and I decide we will use pieces of Veronica's dress under a lace overlay. "It's nice Veronica sent some of her personal items to you before the wedding. I would give anything to have my mother's diary," my friend says.

After my first dress fitting, Alex and I meet with Pierre, the owner of La Coupole, a French restaurant just outside downtown Denver. Not only does Pierre give us the same attention he would give to visiting French dignitaries, he pours four glasses of Laurent Perrier Champagne and summons his assistant, Laetitia, to join us. A kind of vapor passes between Pierre and Laetitia. Well, it's not surprising to see a little sexual tension in the air between two French people in a French restaurant. Just watching the two of them interact causes me to run my tongue around my dry mouth before I take another sip of Champagne.

"Would you like cheese and a baguette to accompany the Champagne, Diane and Alex?" asks Laetitia.

Pierre and Laetitia put together a tantalizing menu for our wedding dinner.

Foie Gras Au Torchon

Vichyssoise

Beet Salad with Creme Fraiche

Roasted Milk Fed Veal Chop

Seasonal Vegetables

Yellow wedding cake with Chantilly between the layers,

topped with ganache frosting and edible flowers

Just as the wedding plans are falling into place, the conference room I use for classes is closing for a renovation. After countless hours of searching for a new location, we are forced to change some of the dates for classes. All of this turmoil causes us to postpone our wedding. I feel exhausted just thinking about rearranging everything, but my daughter, Michelle, who could be a wedding planner, takes care of all the schedule changes.

July 22, 1999, is a hot day. Our wedding ceremony in La Coupole's garden begins with Alex reading a poem:

"Senses" by Alex Glassman

My splendid bouquet of ripe golden roses

Sat on the window ledge waiting for you,

The perfume enticing sins that supposes

The one coming near craves this rendezvous.

The succulent peaches at just the right firmness

Sat on the window ledge bursting for you,

The mouthwatering rapture of sweet little juices

Tempted the tempter with the fragrance of dew.

"Diane, will you marry me."

"Alex, I believe that you love me as I am. I promise to love you as you are. I do. I mean, I will."

The reception begins with a jazz quartet. As soon as the main course is served, the musicians take a break. My son, Craig, steps in front of the instruments to make a wedding roast:

The top 10 reasons Diane saw a psychic before she agreed to marry Alex:

10. Will she have to stop doing romance ads?

9. Will she make a decision about her dress?

8. Will her hairdresser pick the right red dye?

7. Will her makeup artist make her look forty?

6. Will she have to tell Alex her real age?

5. Will she miss her other boyfriends?

4. Will she go to confession before the wedding?

3. Will she make out with the priest?

2. Will she ask the priest to do the ceremony?

1. Will her wedding vows sound sincere?

Raise your glasses, everyone, to Diane and Alex!

Although I asked Craig to roast me, I feel some concern about how shocked my four brothers look. Since they all live on the East Coast, they didn't have details about my dating spree after my divorce and before I met Alex. Fortunately they did laugh during the roast like most of the guests.

"Thanks, Craig! Since Alex read his beautiful poem earlier, I have something to say before the dancing starts. Love is awful! It keeps me awake at night, it makes me curse, it makes me become obsessed about where to put my love. I found the right place to put my love. With you, Alex."

After our guests leave the reception, Alex remembers he left his backpack at the barber's that morning. "Babe, the backpack has both of our passports and all of our foreign money. We won't be leaving the country if the backpack doesn't show up!"

Bless his heart, Alex's barber brings the backpack to us later that night. After the scare, I decide to be involved in our honeymoon plans—not typical for a Diva like me. I prefer to delegate tasks like keeping track of passports, scheduling day trips, etc. My positive attitude, gut instincts, and charm will get me what I want, when I want it, or someone's ass will get kicked!

The truth is, no one is really in charge during the trip, and one of us loses something or gets lost every day. I start missing my ex, who used to take care of everything, including packing my clothes.

We step off the plane at Charles de Gaulle Airport on a rainy Sunday morning in July. I feel at home in the City of Love. Paris is one big work of art. The buildings are magnificent! It's the most amazing city in the world. I roll down my window to hear the city sounds and feel the pulse of French energy. Alex makes groaning sounds about the French air: "a touch moldy, too dusty," he complains.

Who is this guy I married? Is he a male version of Goldilocks—this bed is too soft, this bed is too hard? As we continue to Saint Germaine, I begin to wonder if this honeymoon really will be the honeymoon I need and deserve.

Our room isn't ready at Relais Laetitia. Perhaps some guests are delaying an expedition today, choosing to sleep in and catch a later breakfast buffet on a rainy Sunday morning. A small cafe close by offers us shelter and a great view of Saint Germaine. As we sip cafe creme and eat buttered baguettes, things start to unfold in front of us.

An older woman wearing a cobalt and scarlet cotton dress balances a newspaper and a baguette in her right hand while walking her dog. Her large blue umbrella is in her left hand. When the rain stops, the woman lays out a plastic mat between two popular tourist shops. Turns out, she's a well-dressed beggar, looking more put together than I do. Next, a street cleaner dressed in a lime green nylon vest and matching wide-legged pants arrives with a lime green broom to sweep the sidewalks in front of the storefronts. Alex takes out his camera to capture the brightly colored storefronts on the empty streets while I chat with an American writer who spends one month a year writing in Paris. The owner of the cafe seems to know her well. When the writer hands me her business card, I wonder if she's famous.

After the writer and I talk for a while, she says, "You look at the heart and soul of the city. Perhaps you should write a French mystery. Don't worry, you'll find ways to do what you truly love. Paris has a way of doing that to you!"

The bar is open when we return to the hotel.

"Madame Morrison, you're back! May I fix you a mimosa?" Jacque, the lounge host, says as he greets me with a kiss on the cheek. Jacque is a gorgeous black man who is polite and ridiculously seductive.

"Your monsieur, will he want a drink too?" he asks.

"Alex is my new husband, Jacque. I'll take a mimosa, but he doesn't drink in the morning."

Jacque looks at me with his deep black eyes as if to say a man who doesn't have a drink on a Sunday morning doesn't know the meaning of *dimanche* in Paris. Alex steps out of the elevator looking very American in his jeans and tee. I watch him sweep the lobby area, taking in all of the oil paintings, which are mostly portraits. He takes several photographs, the last one of Jacque and me standing by the open bar.

The next day I lure Alex into going clothes shopping. There's a sale at Le Bon Marche, my favorite department store, or as I call it: a museum of delights. I picture Alex in loose linen pants, colorful linen shirts, and man scarves, but Alex prefers to read a book while sitting on a bench outside the store.

French women are hard-core bargain hunters. I put my hand on a burgundy *sack*, the French term for purse. A woman dressed from head to toe in black Chanel grabs it right out of my hand, then she's gone.

"Merci," I say, which throws the woman off because she doesn't understand my sous-texte, the joke behind my response. She doesn't hand over the purse, but does offer me a cigarette. Being in a store entirely filled with French women makes it easy for me to act like a Diva. I spray myself with N'Aimez que Moi, which means *Love Only Me*. The sales woman gift wraps it and I don't stop her. It is a gift for myself.

Alex is moody this morning. He's not enticed by perfumes I had sprayed on different parts of my body, nor is he annoyed by my five shopping bags full of clothes from the most expensive stores in Paris. Maybe he feels the intensity of being married, since it is a first for him. The sex is definitely less spontaneous on our honeymoon. These things can happen when expectations are too high. I decide to skip analyzing him—I just want to have fun!

Thank God I have Jacque to pour my drinks every night. I'm regretting that the honeymoon continues on to Rouen, north of Paris, tomorrow. I won't have Jacque to flirt with me there. I had one husband who stalked me; now I have one who ignores me. I can almost hear my lawyer Larry warning me I should have done a prenuptial for my second marriage, damn it!

18

Dancing Crones

The moon rises full and burns bright yellow the night we arrive in Rouen. Alex and I walk from the train station to our small rental. The air is full of the fragrance of July gardens. There's a red fox scampering through a field close by as night birds flock toward one of the largest Gothic cathedrals in northern France.

Our home for the next few nights has stone floors, eggplant-purple walls, and window shutters covered with chipped, green paint. There's a large, yellow plate with a black evil eye hanging above the stone fireplace. Alex lights a few candles in Calvados bottles covered with candle drippings. Neither one of us has heard of Calvados brandy. In the meantime, I take a look in the refrigerator, which is stocked with white wine, butter, and cheese: the necessities of rural France. Alex is drawn to the built-in shelves that display a variety of books about Monet's paintings of the Cathedrale de Notre Dame in the middle of town. I'm more interested in the small animal skulls, bird's nests, and bisque statues of Saint Joan of Arc situated between the books. When Alex reads a sweet Monet quote— "I must have flowers always, and always"—I nod my head because I too love flowers.

Right now I'm craving food more than flowers. I grab a piece of cheese, pour myself a glass of wine, and dig into the guest book.

My wife and I became big fans of the local brew, Calvados brandy, which is made from apples and aged in oak casks. We suggest you visit the orchards around Rouen and sample the brandy. But wait to buy Calvados from the dancing crones in the middle of the square.

If you look on the top shelf of the linen closet, you will find a wooden box with a small bottle of Calvados and four shot glasses. Drink the magical brew before you turn in for the night.

After several shots of Calvados, I end up singing Irish tunes and howling along with the night animals. I attempt to write a few words of one of the songs on a paper napkin. I feel my breathing slow and keep writing as my eyes slowly close. Alex carries me to bed, claiming my sexy writing is a turn-on. Calvados must have brought on the dream I remember from that night.

My father was floating around in my yellow and white bedroom where his Purple Heart and Silver Star were displayed. Robert looked more like an angel than a real person. I called on him when things got rough in Jersey City.

"Master," I heard myself say in the dream, "protect me from the drunks tonight." My grandmother, Addie, came into the dream to remind me there are all kinds of masters, and she crossed my forehead with holy oil.

"Why are you taking time to put olive oil on your forehead, Diane? Did you have a weird dream last night? Let's go, babe, the light on the Cathedrale de Notre Dame is perfect."

My favorite personal quote—"If a little is good, more is better"—should include a warning about hangovers. A glass of celery juice, Addie's hangover cure, would help my pounding headache now, but I settle for a cup of black coffee.

When I walk through the massive double doors of the cathedral, my eyes are full of the images that inspired Monet's paintings. Paintings both sacred and profane hang on the oyster-white walls. Prisms of color pour in through the stained-glass windows as I head down the central aisle of the naive.

After lighting three tall candles, I turn to look at a young man chanting while he dances in front of the ornate altar. The sound echoes, causing me to spin around in a rhythm that matches the dancer's. When he stops, he says to me, "Le pardon est abandonne tout espoir d'avoir eu un autre passe different." *Forgiveness is giving up all hope of having had a different past.*

Looking back at the cathedral visit, I realize I released some of the painful times in my life there. I understand why I became a Diva and why letting go of the past is my key to freedom.

My sense of awe continues outside the cathedral, a massive structure with its lacy, rough texture and tall, iron spires. Monet did over thirty finished paintings, as well as many studies, of the exterior. It was typical for him to spend up to six months working on ten canvases at a time, capturing the cathedral in different light. One of his biographers states that the artist dreamed that the cathedral would fall on him someday.

Alex and I continue on to the central square where Joan of Arc was burned at the stake in 1412. My gut wrenches as I imagine this eighteen-year-old girl being set on fire. I yell out "stop" before I know I'm yelling. It's as if I'm back in the 1400s trying to stop Joan from joining the army. I want to tell her the English are going to make an example of her and she will die.

Alex is used to me being eccentric and outspoken. I blame my outburst on a hangover and lack of food. "Let's get some food into you, my sexy protester."

As we move past the square, we see a group of gypsies huddled together on this crisp July morning. The old women cackle as they hold their mugs of black coffee with gnarled, witchy fingers. Their faces are dotted with clumps of dirt. The sound of their collective voices, scratchy from years of smoking, draws a crowd of curious tourists.

There's something sexy about being a crone. Unattached freedom defines them. I look forward to a time when I can breathe more deeply, watch more carefully, dance more often, and shed my Diva mask. As I watch these women dance, I conclude that anyone who defies the conventions of society —gypsies, entertainers, musicians, artists, and speakers—have an inner power that drives them. We can all be Divas! We can all be celebrities! The gypsies have a certain flair. Aging seems natural to them. I feel the energy of their ripening and want that kind of freedom for myself.

Years later, I will reach back to what I learned from the crones when I watch my fiery red hair turn gray and my skin turn pale during a long quarantine.

What causes an audience of tourists to have even a crackle of interest in these gypsies? Is it that they wish they could live outside the box like them? Do they secretly want their chosen freedom?

The gypsies sell their products in between dancing for a growing audience. It is easy for them to sell because they take time to greet each potential buyer. When someone in the audience buys a pendant or their own brand of Calvados, it's as if the buyer gets a piece of the gypsy life to take home.

Each day, millions of us earn our keep by performing. Performers may use their craft on stage, in posh offices, or in tents. There may be years of preparation or very little at all. All good performers create a desire among an audience to let them in.

I pause for a moment to think about how I perform as an educator. It's an exchange. I perform, the teacher takes in my performance, and then adds some of my style to his or her own teaching method.

Before we leave the gypsy camp, Alex photographs the crones standing around a wild boar they are curing for future meals. I buy a pendant in the shape of a boar tusk on my way out. Addie would have worn this, along with her tree of life pendant. She would also drink a bottle of their Calvados.

In the midst of remembering the magic of being in France for two weeks, I start to think about my professional life in Denver and the case of Calvados we bring back on the plane along with our luggage. I'm excited to speak to an audience of teachers again. My next class is in three short days.

19

Dealing with Fame

When I return to Denver, my desire is to be more successful while I carve out ways to have more personal time. Desire is what keeps me up at night, trying to figure out how to get from here to there. Desire is what separates a successful business woman from the rest. I have had this desire to be in control of my life since I was five years old. I was too young then to understand I was a natural entrepreneur.

My desire to become wealthy feels like something screaming in my soul. Alex is right alongside me to help me see the big picture, which makes a difference in how we navigate our new lives. Since my career is moving toward being a keynote speaker for large conventions and doing leadership training in school districts around the country, Alex and I talk about creating a special account for buying art, a pursuit I'd in fact adopted while traveling in Rouen a few years earlier. I can't help thinking about Guilleme, who sold us our first piece of art purchased in France.

"I'm Guilleme. I love your turban and sunglasses, madame. Are you an actress?"

"You flatter me, monsieur, where are you from?"

"I'm spending the summer here in Rouen where the cathedrals and Monet's paintings inspire me to paint."

"When can I see your paintings, Guilleme?" I asked, just as Alex stepped up to the juice bar.

Guillaume hung a *be back in an hour* sign in the juice bar window. He locked the door, then the three of us cut across a field to his studio. It was the size of a closet, yet every inch of space was beautiful and efficiently used. Small paintings were hung just under the molding between the white walls and the chipped ceiling, which were painted in French blue. His paints were arranged in order from titanium white to mars black.

"We will take the small one of the Rouen Cathedral," Alex and I said simultaneously.

A tall man with dark black tattoos on his arms and chest walked into the studio. Guillaume looked flushed and lost any awareness we were in the room.

"No worries, Guillaume, we can pick up the painting tomorrow. You can sign the piece before we return. You are going to be famous someday," I said with a giggle.

The next day when we returned to the juice bar, Guillaume wasn't working. His studio was completely empty except for our painting, which was beautifully wrapped with a note attached that said the painting was meant for me. The address for his new studio in Paris was included in the note.

After sending several letters to Guillaume in Paris, to thank him for our first major art purchase, I contacted the owner of the juice bar in Rouen. Apparently Guillaume had a gambling problem. He had to leave France immediately. When I look at his painting now, I feel sad because I fear something bad has happened to him, but my heart tells me I will see him again.

Guillaume's painting and others I later purchased from galleries in France determine the decor in our home over the years. The more we work on the house and garden, the more it seems we are living in a small town in France. We scrape off the old floral wallpaper in the guest room and paint the walls in a color that looks like melted vanilla ice cream. Alex takes over most of the renovating after I take on more speaking positions in Denver and surrounding towns outside the city.

"What time did you come to bed last night, babe? Did you sleep in your jewelry?"

I don't have the heart to tell Alex I was up until dawn, too tired to worry about my jewelry or yesterday's makeup still on my face. I'm starting to burn out because I depend too much on waving my wand like Tinker Bell, ignoring the fact I'm not twenty-five anymore. My sense of urgency about taking on the highest paying speaking engagements is causing me to disintegrate into a compulsive perfectionist instead of being myself—an adventurous Diva. I'm getting too serious, which has never been good for me.

After I get home from a long walk, Alex and I create goals that will give both of us more freedom. He records my three important goals on individual Post-it notes, which we stick on the closet door in my office. I will delegate more courses to the other professors, develop a series of online courses which Michelle will administer, and only commit to keynote speaking engagements that pay a premium rate.

A few days later, I enter the conference room like an Amazonian Diva. The room looks different—not as stark as usual. There are white linen tablecloths on the tables. Fresh flowers and a tall thermos of coffee and French croissants are waiting for me on a desk I use to set up my materials.

Today's course is about being successful by increasing emotional intelligence, the latest hot topic in European schools. My provocative research on the subject gets me into higher paying consulting positions, which fits with one of my new goals. Evidently, there is a growing interest in emotional intelligence in the US in the early 2000s. European countries now require their teachers to integrate emotional intelligence into their curricula at least one hour a day at every grade level, and I'm geared up to get our schools to follow the European model. With 2003 only a month away, Alex and I plan to visit Provence and Paris to gather more information on how the French introduce emotional intelligence into their classrooms.

20

Holidays

The glitter of the holidays can keep anyone in denial about real life, but sometimes something or someone can ruin the festivities, especially a call from my mother.

"So sorry, Mom. We can't make it back for the holidays because of my teaching schedule."

"You're selfish, Diane, a spoiled Diva always thinking of yourself first. It's shameful you're making so much money just standing up and showing off."

"Come on, Mom, you were a Diva! You dressed in nice dresses and wore high heels around the house. You wanted to be successful like me, but you never took risks. Put Dad on the phone, please."

I know Sam, the peacemaker, will make me feel appreciated and loved after another of my mother's verbal assaults. I ask him his opinion about visiting us during the holidays because we can't fly to New York. Sam, doesn't offer opinions easily. Keeping things running smoothly without conflict brings Sam happiness. He is a natural mediator.

"I'll talk to your mother about a compromise, Diane. We could do Christmas here in New York and New Year's in Denver."

"I can pay for the flight, Dad. I'm doing well!"

We both sigh a little before we say goodbye; we both know Veronica isn't flexible.

The only thing I regret about not going to the East Coast that year is that Sam died in the fall the following year. I missed my last Christmas with him.

"Didn't Veronica help with some of the Christmas displays in Macy's when you lived in Jersey City? Tell me about your holidays when you were a kid," Alex asks.

"Okay, get ready for a chaotic Christmas in the house of drunks. You might prefer stories about Christmas in New York, after Veronica married Sam.

It's 1946, the night before Christmas, and all through the house there was drinking, cursing, and a slurred Christmas carol or two. I was almost asleep when Pop came in drunk. He was obviously trying to keep my dog Blackie from barking before he and the dog knocked over the fresh pine tree. Poor Blackie barked louder after he got hit with, not only the Christmas tree, but also a bunch of ornaments that ended up broken on the wooden floor. Someone took my Christmas dog downstairs, and I could hear his paws scratching the wooden staircase.

The Christmas music was still playing when I got up the next morning. Everyone was out cold on the living room floor. As usual, I picked up beer cans and wiped up the floor where some cans had fallen over. We could never have carpet in our apartment because of the constant beer spills.

Addie thanked me for helping out and, in return, she let my puppy out of the big cardboard box where he had spent the night. After I put my red velvet coat and matching hat on Blackie, I went for a short walk while Addie made carrot and celery juice. She claimed it was good for a hangover, which everyone in the house except me would have.

When Blackie and I returned, my mother was still crashed out on the couch and never knew I left the apartment without her permission."

I can tell by Alex's face he's sorry he asked about my weird childhood. It's not something I like to dwell on, either. In fact, I repressed most of my childhood memories until I was in my fifties. I'm more likely to have one foot in the future, sometimes missing the present, but definitely avoiding the past.

Alex changes the subject, taking me into the present details of what he calls a nice old-fashioned Christmas with a fresh-cut Christmas tree. After lunch, when the temperature is decent and the sun is bright, we head to the mountains to get a tree.

The tree Alex and I cut and drag through the woods is taller than our eleven-foot ceiling in the living room. I have to stand on a ladder to reach the top of the tree. I manage to get sap on my wool sweater, which makes me laugh because I usually freak out when anything happens to my designer clothes, but it's Christmas. I don't have to be a Diva all the time. The whole experience of getting the tree and setting it up brings forth a combination of me cursing and Alex singing Christmas carols.

After we string multicolored lights on the giant tree, we stop for whiskey over ice served in tall glasses decorated with Christmas bells. "Tis the season!" Alex says as we clink glasses.

Veronica had given us some of her collection of Christmas decorations and a white bisque manger which ends up on our fireplace mantel. My mother's old, silver garlands along with plug-in cream-colored candles finish the windows. Finally, I place the vintage ornaments, decorated with something that looks like sugar, on the tree.

After the holidays are over, I walk through my neighborhood, stopping here and there to photograph the remains of outdoor decorations. My hands rub across a pine garland on a fence outside a cafe in the neighborhood. After drinking an Americano and writing some Christmas memories in my journal, I check out the latest art exhibit by a young female artist who lived in Paris before moving to Denver. I purchase one of her paintings of a merry-go-round in the Tuileries Garden for Alex. When I finish reading the artist's biography, I realize I want more time to be creative. Yes, I'm successful, wealthy, and happy, but I need to figure out a way to have creative goals in 2008.

As Alex and I become more familiar with galleries in Denver and San Francisco, we realize we want to collect artists we've met at openings. Their hands have touched the work. I feel as if I have a sense of the artist's spirit in the paint that covers their canvases. Many of the artists we collect say when they paint they are in a state of flow and lose all sense of time. A collector simply cannot get those vibes without having a face-to-face connection with the creator.

21

Provence

I know Alex would rather go to an ashram surrounded by green meadows and quiet than to take another trip to France. Since neither quiet nor green fields appeal to me, we book a trip to Avignon in Provence. The truth is, I prefer paintings of green meadows and loud bars.

The chateau where we plan to stay is twenty minutes from Gare d'Avignon. Avignon is the home of the Palais de Papes and some of the best restaurants south of Paris. When we arrive in mid-September of the following year, I begin researching when the papacy moved from Rome to Avignon.

Soon, I'm gazing at the vineyard on the grounds of Chateau Regina. Betina and Aad, the owners, and their dogs, Sushi and Sasa, greet us just outside the main door. We proceed to an apartment, separate from the main house, where we'll be staying for a week. There's a bottle of Aad's Chateau Red on a small, metal cafe table that sits in front of a large glass door. The violet grapes hang heavy on the vines a stone's throw from our patio. I feel intoxicated looking at them. Alex claims it's jet lag, but I disagree. Nonetheless, I'm not moving from the view.

Fortunately, we don't have to leave the chateau tonight. Our apartment is more like a small house with a fully-equipped kitchen, dining room, sitting room, master bedroom, and a bathroom with a large sunken tub and a full marble shower. I could live here!

Alex pours Aix Rosé into heavy, pink wine glasses. We like to drink wine when we cook a meal together. Tonight the menu includes couscous with lamb and steamed asparagus purchased from an open market in Avignon. I'm in charge of preparing the couscous Moroccan style, which involves steaming and plumping the grain with my hands three times. Alex holds a wine glass to my mouth so I can still drink because my hands are sticky. I watch him add ginger, cinnamon, coriander, paprika, black pepper, and the lamb shanks to the lamb broth before he steams the asparagus.

I remove Betina's apron before dishing the food onto heavy French dinner plates painted with large-stemmed artichokes. The meal looks like a work of art.

"Now the Champagne. Cheers to you, madame."

"To you, monsieur. I didn't see you purchase the bubbly."

Our first evening turns into a combination of French jazz and small talk until the night sounds begin: crickets, cicadas, and owls. Just as we're ready for our dessert of verbena-flavored ice cream, Alex hears what he thinks must be the sound of wild boar hooves crashing through the brush close to the chateau. Aad had warned us there were boars running rampant in Provence this fall. We hear their zombie noises—snorting, heavy breathing, and primitive growling.

Alex grabs his camera, and I grab a flask of whiskey. Aad had shot a male boar recently, and its belly was jam-packed with grapes. That boar is being cured in a storage room on the grounds, but tonight's visitor gets away, which disappoints Aad.

"Why do boars wait until the grapes are so ripe, Aad?" I ask him afterward.

"Nature has provided a pleasurable way for boar to propagate. The tannins in ripe grapes make them horny." Aad picks a handful of grapes for Alex and me and laughs so loud several lights go on in the guest rooms. Before we all turn in for the night, Aad explains the male boar might return later to gather food for his young.

"You might see him by the large fig tree across from your front door. The boar are omnivores. Apparently, the dark figs are a delicacy. Most property owners don't protect the figs like they protect their vineyards, nor do we. The boar only eat the over-ripe ones Betina wouldn't serve to guests."

I suspect Alex lay awake last night, hoping he could photograph a wild boar eating figs. He seems out of sorts this morning, but I'm fired up. Last night was so exciting!

"Ready for the next adventure, Alex? Maybe explore the cave on the edge of the woods before breakfast? Aad tells me he finds boar droppings in the cave once or twice a week."

All I get from Alex is a snort. Later, we walk through the French doors to the dining area in the main house. The *petit dejeuner* Betina set up is five-stars amazing, with meats, cheeses, breads, pastries, fruits, hard boiled eggs, juices, cafe creme, and tea.

Just as we sit down at the long table covered with a yellow provincial print tablecloth, Betina quiets us by placing her pointer finger on her mouth.

"The hunters are coming," Aad says, letting us know this is not typical in the morning but the farmers are tired from dealing with wild boar.

One of the guests mentions that one factor is the increase in acreage dedicated to corn farming in southern France, which is encroaching on the boar's natural habitat and forcing the animals to look elsewhere for food, hence its penchant for grapes and other crops. Hunters call the grape-loving boar *sangliers*, a romantic name for nasty-looking animals.

I leave my food to get a better view of the hunters. There are ten of them wearing bright yellow vests. They hold their guns on the left and keep their bell-wearing dogs on the right.

What if the boar daddy that came down last night gets killed? It doesn't seem right. My blood feels frozen. I have a sense of loathing and some fear about so many hunters on the chateau grounds.

"It's going to be a rainy day, everyone. You might want to stay in to read a book, perhaps do some writing," Betina suggests.

I feel like I'm in a Tarantino movie. Maybe I'll write a mystery titled *Croissants and Murder.* While Alex takes a tour of the main house with Betina, I keep my eye on the hunters. Meanwhile, Aad captivates the guests with stories about living in wild boar country. He actually created bait to lure the boar for the hunters. "Excuse me," he says, "I'm getting a little turned on picturing Betina in a red dress with white polka dots and a big white hat selling my bait at the outdoor market. Come back for my special gin and tonic tonight, folks." He wipes sweat from his brow.

Aad is a hefty Dutchman with a heart of gold, but I do sense the chateau owner wouldn't take crap from anyone. Betina, a former model, dresses in designer clothes every day, even when she's working in the garden. What an interesting couple. Alex and I feel as if we are staying in a small Versailles with the most amiable hosts possible. I am in Diva heaven!

The rain is supposed to end by late afternoon. Since Alex was raised an Orthodox Jew, I suggest we visit a synagogue in the morning. "Did you know Carpentras has the oldest synagogue in France? It's only fifteen minutes away, Alex. We can save the towns that are farther away for this afternoon. Would you like Betina to set up a tour of the synagogue for us?"

Alex argues with me about where to park in Carpentras. He insists on parking on a side street where a collection of *les gens de la rue*, street people, live in small tents.

After Alex parks, he literally runs away from me, causing me to realize once again that my husband isn't completely normal. He's more than eccentric.

I'm aware very few people speak English in Carpentras, and Alex does have the keys to the car and the chateau, as well as my passport. I decide to blaze my own trail today. I walk toward the synagogue, convinced I will have a fabulous time in spite of the rain and Alex's attempt to ruin my day. I almost walk out of a small cafe next to the synagogue when a couple about my age from Toronto invite me to join them. It's amazing what a Quiche Lorraine, a glass of Champagne, and good company can do for a Diva.

I have a wonderful time flirting with the charming tour guide while waiting for Alex to arrive with the tickets. The guide had greeted me with a kiss on each cheek, typical in the south, which gave me the opening I needed to play the game.

"Madame," he says, "you look like Coco Chanel, dressed in such finery. I'm going to have a cigarette. Would you like one?" It's been years since I smoked. The thin French cigarette feels sexy in my mouth.

Alex arrives with a map to the synagogue just before the tour begins. I depended on Betina's verbal directions.

"Monsieur, your wife is very beautiful. You're a lucky man," the guide says. Alex makes another snorting sound, and the guide laughs and offers each of us a pamphlet. Mine has the guide's autograph with his name and phone number inside. He must be twenty years younger than me. So many temptations in France.

The synagogue exhibits a sense of pride and tradition. Alex takes a photo of the prayer room, which features gold walls and a teal blue ceiling that has gold leaf mixed in with the blue paint.

As everyone heads down the monumental staircase to the ground floor, I feel like I'm walking into a mysterious place. The mikvah, or ritual baths, downstairs are mainly used by women after they finish their period. Women are considered to be unclean until they bathe. The separate schedule for men and women is listed on the door.

Two giant ovens close to the mikvah sit empty. I'm curious about the gigantic bread board covered with flour that is in the middle of one of them. I linger downstairs as the tour returns to the first floor. I move the board in the biggest stone oven. A small amount of flour wafts out, covering my face and exposing a small sketch on a scrap of paper. Rather than going further with my inappropriate behavior, I pull my hand out of the oven and plan to ask the guide about the sketch after the tour ends.

"It will be my pleasure to check the mysterious paper for you, madame," the guide says.

I pace the floor as I watch him put gloves on before he uncovers the sketch.

"Oh," he says, "this was done by the Rabbi's youngest. She hides her drawings in secret places. Please, she would be happy for you to have this one. See her tiny initial *M* to the side. Her name is Marie."

I offer to pay for the sketch or send him a cowboy shirt from Denver, but he only accepts a Provincial kiss.

Alex hands me a clean handkerchief to protect my sketch, which I soon frame and place on our gallery wall next to a photo of the guide when we return to Denver. I was hoping the sketch was a stolen piece of art hidden in the old oven for years. Maybe I've been reading too many mysteries about art theft.

When we return to the chateau, Aad is in the midst of inviting all the guests to a gin and tonic happy hour. After I take my fill of the Dutch version of one of my favorite drinks, Aad writes the recipe down for me.

Pour 2 ounces of Monkey 47 gin in stemmed goblet

Add large ice cube

Squeeze 1–3 lime wedges

Add 3–4 ounces tonic

Stir

Garnish with sprigs of rosemary, thyme, sliced cucumber, and candied ginger.

Alex doesn't join us for drinks in the garden. Later, I open the windows as the sun is just starting to set. A sliver of light falls on my body as I finish undressing. I rub myself down with French lavender oil and put on a short, pink satin nightgown, hoping to see the male boar from our back patio later.

Betina mixes up a lime elixir to ease my throat when I sit down for breakfast the next morning. She makes a little a joke about getting hoarse from too much sex.

"Betina, I'm embarrassed to tell you: Alex slept on the couch last night."

The rest of our time in Provence is full of cobalt blue skies and large cumulus clouds. Aad leads a group of us on a trip to Gordes one afternoon. Gordes has one of the most sophisticated markets in Provence. Aad also points out the war memorial in the middle of the town square. Gordes was one of the few towns that was bombed during World War II because it was the center of the resistance against the Nazis in Provence.

After we tour an old church that is tucked away on a tiny lane, Aad points at a large castle in the distance, which he claims is haunted.

"Anyone interested in a bottle or two of pastis before we return to the chateau?" he asks.

We shared happy hour on two benches outside another small church.

"Well!" Aad says. "There are all kinds of spiritual experiences. It's said that more than one pastis in a sitting can result in a stream of consciousness conversation about life and its many hardships. As the French say, *C'est une vie difficile*. Remember to always mix one part water with one part pastis. I don't want you to have a bad hangover," he laughs.

After five days in Provence, we return to Gare de Lyon in the middle of a train strike. At least five different languages are spoken at the station. I can tell by the tone of people's voices and their hand movements that their conversations are about the strike.

"How are we going to exit the station without crossing the strike?" I ask a young French man close to me.

"Don't worry. You should be able to proceed soon. Americans think that our sirens signal attacks. This one means more strikers are coming down to the main floor. See them in their bright green vests on the second floor? They will start to yell, beat drums, and blow horns soon. We strike before we negotiate in France."

Instead of getting stressed by the hullabaloo of the strike, I dance to the loud music. Then I coax Alex to go to the upper level of the station to have a glass of Champagne at the magnificent restaurant, Le Train Bleu, one of my favorite restaurants in Paris.

I splash myself with water in the restaurant lounge before I call an Uber, but I still apologize to the driver for working up such a sweat at the Gare.

After I take a shower at Relais Laetitia, Alex watches me dress in my black linen skirt, sage green linen blouse, and rose silk scarf. He remarks that my new straw hat accents my fair skin as we start our first of two days in Paris. "I remember what a hit you were at the market in Provence, babe. As soon as you put tonight's outfit on in the vendor's tent, you looked like a French Diva. I can still see you dancing with the jazz band at the end of the market and remember how a crowd gathered around you and made you dance longer. Applause works in any language."

Alex, who has a photographer's eye, sees much more than I imagine sometimes. It rarely flatters me, I'm not sure why, but it could be I flatter myself so much. The thing is, Alex comes alive when I act like a Diva. No matter how anyone interprets *Diva*—performer, show-off, or strong woman —my husband likes it all.

"Shall we have Jacque pour us a Campari over ice tonight?"

"You go ahead. I'll join you before we leave for Christine. Our reservation is in an hour. The restaurant is next door. Enjoy your time with Jacque."

"Madame Morrison, you're back!"

"Jacque, you're still here."

22

Restoration

Back in Denver and dealing with jet lag, Alex and I walk a couple miles to a French-Korean bakery.

"A brisk walk," I tell Alex, "is one of the best ways to shake the ennui after the red-eye flight home. We gained eight hours, but it doesn't feel like it." We've reached the counter. "I'll take a chai latte with oat milk and a splash of lavender syrup."

"An extra-large cold press coffee for me, merci," says Alex.

"Anything to eat, perhaps a croissant or a fruit tart?"

I can't seem to shake my French addiction to elegant pastries and point to each of our favorites. I'm passionate about the French lifestyle. It takes me at least three weeks to acknowledge I am really in Denver instead of belle France.

My phone trembles in my hand, even though I know that hesitation is a block. Speaking of hesitation, Alex hasn't said one word to me since we left the house. He's being diligent about watching the early morning activity on the other side of Pearl Street.

"John is going into his gallery, Alex. Isn't he usually closed on Mondays?"

Alex nods as he reaches into his backpack. I was wondering why he'd carried it with him.

"Look at this painting I picked up at the open market in San Remy, babe."

When he shows me a 9x12 oil on linen with the vendor's documentation that the piece is at least a thousand years old, I suddenly feel wide awake. It could have been the coffee or the mystery connected with the painting, but I think it was more that Alex kept this secret the whole time we were in Provence.

When I hold the painting up to the light, I see at least six layers of paint on the canvas. Some of the edges have chipped off, making it easy to see what's under each layer. The vendor had told Alex that linen was very expensive in the early 1700s. Artists would often paint over their canvases many times to save the cost of buying new linen.

Alex says he'd made an appointment with our friend John this morning.

"So that's why you kept looking across the street, and why John is in the gallery on his day off. Aren't you sneaky, Alex!"

John, who restores and sells European paintings from the eighteenth and nineteenth centuries, thinks our small piece might be very valuable. He estimates that our painting was done in the late 1700s toward the end of Johannes Vermeer's life, possibly by the artist himself.

John covers the first layer of the painting with a combination of linseed oil, toxic botanicals from France, and a small amount of cheap gin. The painting bubbles up while the three of us catch up on our lives. When the bubbling stops, John uses a squeegee to take off the first layer. I guess we are lucky because John doesn't have to use a scraper to get to the second layer.

After several days spent removing the top four layers, John swears he has uncovered a study that looks similar to Vermeer's "Girl with a Red Hat."

John suggests that if the piece is an authentic Vermeer study, it was probably done by the artist's daughter Maria. It could be one of many primitive studies by Maria; it's estimated that she did twenty percent of her father's paintings, and possibly "Girl with a Red Hat," which is in the National Gallery in Washington, DC.

"This calls for a celebration," I say, doing a little dance in John's studio, "Maybe we have a masterpiece on our hands. If we do have a valuable painting, Alex and I could sell it and move to France." The coffee table in the living room has been covered with photographs of Paris for days. The first photo I pick up is of me placing a single red rose on Edith Piaf's grave in Pere Lachaise Cemetery.

I remember the elderly caretaker in one of the photos who had a snapshot of Piaf in his hand when Alex took his picture. My French isn't good enough to ask the gentleman why he pointed at me with tears in his eyes.

"He thinks you look like Piaf."

"I hope I never look as sad as the French cabaret singer, who the caretaker was clearly enamored with."

When Alex points to a photograph of a young child standing by Oscar Wilde's grave, my mind drifts off to when I stood in front of my father's grave in Green-Wood Cemetery as a child.

I sometimes wonder if Robert was a Hustler, the male version of a Diva. Robert went to Julliard School of Music and played in a band called Mitchell Ayres. My father was not only rich, he was classy, intelligent, charming, and funny.

My son, Craig, found out Robert played in strip joints before he got into Mitchell Ayres. Oddly, this fact is more important to me than all of his war medals and commendations because it helps me accept my tendency to live outside the box.

A week after our return from Paris, Alex and I attend a funeral for an artist friend of ours. During the service, my mind wanders off.

Pop offered me a handful of chocolates to shut me up the day of my father's funeral. I threw them on the floor and kept on yelling, "I want to go!"

I was not allowed to go to Robert's funeral. He'd been killed two years ago, but his body wasn't sent home from Germany until two years later. I wanted to touch the American flag Pop told me would be wrapped around the casket.

Eventually Pop ignored my screaming and throwing pillows at my babysitter. He just continued on, leading Veronica to a cab waiting outside. My babysitter calmed me down after she asked me if I saw my mother crying. I remember Veronica's eyes were swollen that day.

Alex pulls me from my reverie when we stop at a bar on the way home. I'm embarrassed to tell him I've never been to a funeral. Funerals are such a farce, way too much hullabaloo. I certainly don't want one myself. I'd prefer to have my ashes sprinkled somewhere in France.

"Do you feel alright? You look flushed, babe."

"A bit sozzled. I just need a nap."

23

The Blue Room

I'm sitting in the Blue Room, turning here and there to enjoy our paintings and the French garden. So much comes up here. What a crazy life this has been: this life as a Diva, seductress, Amazonian woman. I love these parts of myself.

Wasn't it Walt Whitman who said we all have multitude selves in one amazing Self? I have learned that some of these parts don't match up—they contradict. I'm a Diva, but I could have been a monk in a far-off jungle monastery. How does one make sense of all these different parts? All we can be is who we are meant to be. In fact, I fondly recall a Benedictine monk telling me that at a retreat in Aspen twenty years ago.

I take a sip of tequila as I catch sight of a robin landing on our peach tree. The robin flitters away; she's gone. I look around this room. It means so much to me. I do so many meaningful things here: writing, painting, and making love. I had the room painted blue ten years ago. Why did I choose blue? I love that Krishna is blue. Picasso had a blue period. Blue is oh so French!

In the midst of all this beauty, I face the truth. I'm addicted to success. Ambitious Divas like myself tend to get sick as soon as they have time to get sick, which is exactly what happened to me.

The Carrera marble fireplace contrasts well with the French blue walls in my bedroom. There's a warmth and charm about the Blue Room. A six-candle crystal chandelier hangs in the middle of the embossed eleven-foot ceiling. An easel with a blank canvas sits in the corner of the room.

What do you do when the room that normally inspires you becomes dark and threatening? I focus on the painting in clear sight: a nude rising up from dark water at sunrise. Half of her face is obscured by something that looks like sunlight.

I start coughing and spitting up chunks of mucus. Then I hear a masculine voice say, "Release fear." I'm hallucinating. The longer I stare at the colors in the painting, blue becomes black and black becomes blue. The figure steps off the canvas to greet me. I'm in a state of ennui as I attempt to get out of bed to touch her. I try my emergency asthma spray again, a shot of Cognac, and put my hand-warmers on my chest. My lack of oxygen makes everything in the room nebulous. Sweat pours down my back. I must have a fever.

It seems I have the kind of illnesses I had as a young child. I had pneumonia twice in six months when I was five years old. I missed almost my entire year of kindergarten.

Thank God, I remember a friend telling me the best way to calm down during an asthma attack is to breathe in through my nose three times then breathe out through my mouth three times. I check my pulse. I can tell my blood pressure is going down.

Once my breathing improves, I make a cup of hot tea with honey and open the shades to get a glimpse of the garden in the early dawn light. Everything in life is about time. Time seems frozen this morning. My work schedule keeps me aware of chronological time, always aware of what's urgent, often missing what's important.

I grab my coat and shoes. My feet need to touch the ground outside. My hands sweep across the soft-leafed bushes that remain green all year. Dora, my psychic, once told me liminal time, between dawn and early morning, is the best time to make it through a rite of passage. Could the asthma attack move me closer to finding my authentic self?

Remembering the message about releasing fear earlier helps me get the courage to call my brother Jack.

"Jack, I've been such a damn Diva all my life. Forgive me for not staying in touch with you because I've been so focused on being successful. I'm sorry I didn't defend you against Veronica's abuse when we were kids. I have some guilt. I didn't talk to Sam about the things Veronica did to you. Call me back. I love you! Diane."

I climb back into bed, expecting to cuddle up to Alex's warm body, but he must have already moved to the guest room. He's paranoid about getting sick.

I want to find out who I am under my Diva mask, but I've only had three hours sleep and Jack called back later that morning. "You did stand up for me, sis. You were the only one of us who could confront Veronica. I can still hear you telling her to give me a break, over and over. We were more than brother and sister. We were best buddies."

"I'm scared, Jack, my ego is a bitch to tame. You know how I love my sports cars, designer clothes, and fancy restaurants. I'm struggling with having wealth. What if my authentic self likes consignment clothes, used cars, and fast food?"

Jack laughs. "There's nothing wrong with being a Diva. I'm not sure about this *authentic self* stuff."

After breakfast, I take one of my canvases out of storage. My creative side is longing for attention today. When I finish painting, I'll schedule an appointment with Professor Charles at his Boulder studio. He's always objective about my work.

"There are layers of emotion in this painting, Diane. Depression is topped with anger. Anger is topped with love. The clouds above the figure have a magnetic pull. Is she being pulled into the clouds, or are the clouds releasing her to remain on the ground?" he asks.

"I'm painting the images from my unconscious, Charles. I sit with the work and wait for it to say something to me. It's like a love affair. I give myself to the work, whether I'm painting on an easel or on the floor. I use brushes, sticks, turkey basters—whatever I can find to move the juicy pigments onto the canvas."

"You're still a demure Diva in a provocative way. Your spiritual side is becoming more clear in the new paintings. Never forget, Diane, you became an artist during your cancer experience when you made those primitive pastel sketches. Those sketches are still in you, Diane. Let that energy continue to show in your new work. I'm glad you're painting again. Call me when you return from NYC."

Charles is romantic and sensitive. His critique of my painting is intuitive. It's easy for me to express my emotions with him, and I let him know I appreciate the fact he can share his emotions with me.

24

Green-Wood Cemetery

"Nothing is forever, except change," I whisper as I look out the window in the lobby of the James Hotel. The clouds are ominous. It's going to be a rainy day. I think about visiting Robert's grave in Brooklyn after thirty years.

The cemetery was a park when I was a little girl. Tilly, my grandmother, took me there to visit Robert's grave. Later, I would dance amongst the trees, singing songs or reciting nursery rhymes. She brought sandwiches, homemade chocolate chip cookies, and chocolate milk for lunch. We sat on our favorite bench away from headstones.

Knowing my experience in Green-Wood will be different today, I pretend I am one of the professionals rushing to work in black business suits. I would flag down a taxi rather than deal with running to a subway station like they are.

"Madame, may I refresh your coffee and bring you a pastry? The James has sweets delivered from Balthazar, one of the best bakeries downtown. I'm Louis, I saw you at Salmagundi Club last night. The featured artists all knew you. Do you collect all of them?"

"Monsieur, I must return to my writing. I have a deadline."

After Louis left the lobby, I'm sorry I didn't have at least a short conversation with him. He seemed like a nice man. I probably shouldn't have worn my sexy night clothes in the lobby expecting to go unnoticed. The truth is, I felt embarrassed when Louis approached me.

I watch Louis run toward Chelsea Market in his Mark Weldon black running pants, long sleeve white Oakley tee, and a duckbill hat from Patagonia. Oh God, he's taking his shirt off. Damn it, I should have let him hit on me! Why can't I find a personal trainer like him?

I wonder what Louis has upstairs in his closet: running shoes that are color-coded and arranged according to his likes and dislikes and patterned shirts with large flowers. He probably loves denim but only wears black pants when in NYC.

"Would you like me to bring you a cup of coffee and a pastry, Alex? I've been talking to an interesting man in the lobby who saw us at the opening last night. I must have had too much Champagne because I don't remember him at all."

"You look sexy in that satin gown, babe. Your lingerie is appropriate to wear in public. Put the red Prada heels and the turquoise sunglasses on. I want you to pose for me on the navy Queen Anne chair. I'll take a few shots of you before I get dressed."

"Only if I can take a shot of you in that big hotel towel. You're soaking wet!"

Alex entertains me with a history lesson on our way to the cemetery. "Green-Wood Cemetery became a popular tourist attraction in the 1830s. The cemetery was so popular that urban planners challenged architects to come up with plans for a separate greenspace for Manhattan. That is how Central Park and Prospect Park were born."

"Let's look at it as a park today. You can roam around with your camera. There are many famous people buried in Green-Wood. I'm sure you will want to photograph Tiffany's grave."

The cab drops us very close to my father's grave. Green-Wood Cemetery looks like a nice place to lie on the way to eternity. Robert's headstone is surrounded by obelisks, draped urns, statues of gothic women, and one grave decorated with an empty bottle of Grey Goose vodka. I watch Alex pretend he's taking a slug.

As we get closer to Robert's grave, I swear I can hear grandma Addie telling me how she prepared our apartment for mourning after the fateful telegram about my father's death arrived. I covered the mirrors with black crepe paper so Robert wouldn't see his own reflection, which would keep him closer to the earth. I also detached the pendulum of the tall clock, signifying the hour his life ended.

The gravestone reads: Robert Vicars Morrison, died in action October 8, 1945.

Kissing the gravestone is an old Irish tradition. My hand gets tangled in my black onyx Tiffany necklace as I kiss my father's name. Beads scatter everywhere. I leave the beads, liking the symbolism of an expensive necklace strewn across my father's grave.

"The truth is, Robert, I wish you could have been my knight in shining armor instead of a war hero. I'm strong. Always have been. I overcame many hard things in my life, but it would have been easier if you had been by my side."

A large panel of light comes through a grouping of trees as I imagine Robert walking through the bloody fields of Aachen, Germany. My father saved a young soldier's life. Both men were shot. My father died, the young man lived. Robert's Silver Star, Purple Heart, and written commendations never meant anything to me. I gave all of the memorabilia to my son.

Robert means something to me, but I would rather think of him as a talented, eccentric man than a war hero.

October 25, 1945

Dear Veronica,

I am so very sorry for your loss. When Robert and I were together before he left for Germany, he successfully discharged duties commensurate with a much higher rank than he held. I hope that I have succeeded in some way to let you know the deep respect and admiration I had for your husband. Although your grief overshadows everything else, you should take strength from the fact that Bob's supreme sacrifice helped to speed total victory for our cause.

Major William Archibald

I read the Major's letter, along with other letters from men who called Robert a crooner because he sang Frank Sinatra songs on the field. Then I put everything back in a metal box before leaving Green-Wood.

Robert lived a charmed life before he was drafted. He was impetuous, a trickster, a risk taker, and a rebellious rule-breaker. He attended Juilliard School of Music. Robert was playing the drums in a joint outside Jersey City when he first saw Veronica. His sister, Marjorie, told me Robert fell in love with my mother the night they met. He was dating Nancy Barbato, Sinatra's cousin, at the time. Nancy was the first of many of Frank's wives and lovers.

Robert invited Veronica and her two cousins out for drinks after his last set. Veronica declined because she had to go to Mass the next day. I imagine he must have known that falling in love with a Catholic would not go over well with his strict Protestant parents. Protestants and Catholics didn't intermarry in the forties. My mother and father married against both parent's wishes. That decision framed my early life because the Harpers, who we lived with after Robert died, kept me from the Morrisons. The Harpers were afraid the Morrisons would take me away from Veronica and raise me Protestant. In addition, the Harpers, who struggled to put bread on the table, resented the aristocratic, wealthy Morrisons.

I'm missing much of Morrison history, although I'm more a Morrison than a Harper.

25

Memories

We're close to 44 Prospect Avenue, Robert's home growing up. All the living room windows were covered with dusty, gray drapes. My grandfather was claiming the world was coming to an end. That was why the basement was always full of cases of food.

The basement was not much darker than the rest of the house. I went down there to gather cans of fruits and vegetables for Tilly. Tilly let me remove my favorite labels, the ones with bright red tomatoes over a turquoise background. My grandmother and I made sketches of the labels. She would always smile when she was being creative. Tilly was depressed. Art was her only therapy.

I slept on a twin bed covered with a blanket that looked like an American flag in Robert's music room.

"We're here!" Alex announces.

There's a Keller Williams *For Sale* sign on the front lawn. The realtor pulls up just as I write down the information about the property. Peggy looks good in her power colors: bright red pants suit, black silk blouse, red-soled Louboutin heels that match her black, crossbody Chanel purse.

"I'm Diane Morrison. My father Robert grew up in this house. Are you having an open house today? My husband Alex and I would love to see the inside."

Peggy puts up the *Open House* sign and forewarns me the property has a contract pending. The house looks fresh and modern, with light pouring in from all directions. The realtor mentions one of my family members helped the former owner redesign the house. It has to be my uncle William, an architect and designer.

As people arrive, I find myself giving small commentaries about each room. I have a tendency to think everyone is interested in what I have to say.

"You do have a way of bringing people together," Peggy says. "Have you ever thought about being a realtor? You're a charismatic Diva, probably able to sell anything."

While Peggy finishes up with a serious client, I go back up to my father's music room, which looks almost the same as it did in the fifties. I feel close to my father. I had tried to explain to my mother that sometimes I felt like Robert was inside me trying to get out. Carl Jung would have had a heyday with that idea.

My aunt Marjorie told me she was physically thrown across the living room when Robert was shot. They were that connected. Marjorie said my father carried a picture of me in his pocket. Was there blood on my picture when he was shot? Who carried him off the field after he fell to the ground? Did he know he was a hero?

I have to stop for a shot of whiskey after Peggy confirms 44 Prospect Avenue is sold.

"Would you really like a second home in Brooklyn?" Alex asks.

"Are you kidding me, Alex? The top art galleries in the world are located in Manhattan and Brooklyn. The thought of shopping in the city anytime I want makes my Diva heart beat faster. Most of my mother's family live in areas just outside of the city. It might be nice to see them more often."

Back to reality in Denver, I wonder if Alex could deal with the stress of having two homes. We discuss buying a place in Brooklyn, but agreed it is something that would cause both of us stress. When I fly back to New York a week later because Sam has suffered a stroke, and two days later the doctors diagnose him with terminal brain cancer, buying a property in Brooklyn seems more like a fantasy than something real.

I'm back in my old New York bedroom, listening to rain pelt against the window. I crack the latch to touch the raindrops like I did when I was young. I moisten my forehead with the rain before checking on Sam. Veronica rarely checks on him. Poor Sam reaches out with his cracked hands. I wash his hands and face with cool lavender water. He smiles when I moisten his hands with cream and put Chapstick on his lips. My father is devastated because he has trouble communicating. The room is eerie without his voice.

Later that night, I take him downstairs to watch *Out of Africa*. Sam loves to smoke when he watches a movie. There's a twinkle in his eye when I light a Marlboro for him. We both know Veronica will have a fit if she catches him.

"Sam is dying of a brain tumor, Veronica. What difference does it make if he has a cigarette?

I help Sam get dressed in his favorite khaki pants and a soft cotton shirt that matches his blue eyes. He reaches for his gray sweater because it's brisk this morning. Our walk is slow today, one foot forward and then the other. He's the child and I'm the parent. Things are reversed.

"Dying," he says, over and over.

When we return, Sam taps on the wooden door three times, as if he's sending a message to someone. Could it be God? "Mean," he cries, as he

162

shows me marks on his wrists. Veronica ties him to the bed when I'm not there.

"I know, Dad. I'm going to get you help. I promise. I will get you a special nurse who will visit you every day. She will make sure Veronica isn't mean to you. Maybe Jerry can step in too. He's a doctor after all!"

"I love you Diane. You are my only daughter," Sam struggles to say.

Then he insists on climbing up a full flight of stairs without help. I clap when he gets to the top. He claps too.

This will be the last time I see my beloved Sam alive.

Just before I leave New York, Veronica threatens to commit suicide because she doesn't want to go to assisted living or a mental hospital. The unconscious is kind; some memories don't surface until we can handle them. When my mother talks about wanting to take pills, I remember another time she tried to overdose.

I was lying in my twin bed in the yellow room with the big white flowers. The small white clock chimed six times. Saint Anne's church bells rang six times. I feel the warmth of my blanket in my cold bed. Hiding under the blanket made me feel safe. My mother's terrible nightmares returned a week before my tenth birthday, November 24, 1952.

A single magpie landed on a windowsill outside our bedroom. When the magpie wouldn't stop tapping on the window, I turned around to look at my mother. Veronica was always sad about losing Robert. She looked in our large oval mirror while she rubbed her body with the olive oil we use on salads. Her body shone like Pop's old car when he waxed it. Veronica continued to look in the mirror, as if she could see Robert behind her. I've never seen his ghost, but she did. After she kissed his photographs and laid a black cloth over his war medals, she grabbed a bottle of pills. Her hand shook so hard she couldn't open the bottle. I grabbed the bottle from her, flushed all the pills down the toilet, and threw holy water in her face. The water ran down her face and down my arm. Sometimes I'd faint when my Mother tried to take pills, but not that night. I concentrated on my feet touching the rough patches of the linoleum floor. I didn't care if the floor scratched the bottoms of my bare feet. I wanted to know that my feet were on the ground. I heard Addie cursing between her false teeth but was happy to see her in the room. By then, I was shaking so hard my knees bumped against each other. Addie told Veronica she'd go straight to hell if she killed herself. Someone in the house called an ambulance, and soon I heard sirens getting closer. The doctors rushed in, put Veronica in a white jacket, and talked to her as if she were a young child.

I put on my red Mary Jane shoes and my red wool winter coat while everyone was paying so much attention to Veronica. I got out of the house without being seen. I listened to my shoes scraping down the fifteen steps as I ran. The same magpie I saw earlier sat on a hedge outside our dark green iron gate.

"Are you a spirit? Do you know my father?"

A light was on in my friend Margaret's kitchen.

Unfortunately, Addie came to pick me up later the following morning. "Thank you for letting Cookie stay with you last night, Margaret. Her mother was lucky—Veronica didn't have to go to the hospital last night."

Before I left Margaret's, I made a joke about how Addie threw raw chickens out the window when she got mad at Pop when he was drunk. Addie looked angry, but she never hurt me.

Now, sixty years later, my mother is again threatening to end her life. Thank goodness my brother Jerry, the doctor, is here from Pennsylvania to finally put Veronica on antidepressants.

"You'll feel much better on the meds, Mom," he says. "Think of a time when you were happy. You will feel like that again soon."

"What would happy look like?" she asks.

All three of us have tears in our eyes.

26

All Kinds of Spiritual Experiences

After watching Sam and Veronica suffer during my visit to New York, I am actually ready to deal with focusing on a spiritual path again.

At dinner, the night of my return to Denver, Alex hands me an invitation to join an exclusive vipassana meditation group. The vipassana group, already established for six months, chose me to join them, stating that my positive attitude about life would bring a sense of happiness to the group.

Okay, Guru Steve must have me confused with another attendee from his silent retreats. I was sure he would ask me to leave during the one-week retreat, I was that obnoxious. Maybe he chalked it up to my Diva personality or, more likely, he thinks I have money. I'll check it out, no cost involved. I try to drag Alex along with me, but he's not interested. Damn it—Alex is the one who got me into vipassana.

Most of my spiritual experiences were connected with churches: the Catholic and the born again Christian. The Catholic Church was all about the saints and the feast days for me. Now my born again Christian route—that was a fiery, almost wild ass religion, with people speaking in tongues. I only speak in tongues when I'm drunk. Falling down in the spirit was relaxing because there would usually be some nice looking guy behind me in case I might end up falling on the floor. Those were the days! Born-againers have great music and damn those ministers can speak! I often ask myself why I didn't stick with those charismatic Bible-quoting group, but no, I seem to want a little stark meditation without even a cool mantra.

Guru Steve's arrangement is comfortable enough—nothing unusual except a Christmas tree strewn with lights he has obviously had up for months. Oh well, I guess he'll be early for the next Yule season. The fireplace is on, candles are lit, and there is a large staff leaning on the wall left of the fireplace. Red and green yoga mats with multi-colored silk pillows are laying on top of a gray plush carpet. The rules of vipassana meditation are posted above the fireplace: *Focus on your breath. Thoughts coming through must be blocked. Let them float through without judgement. Continue to breathe.*

I am feeling slightly enlightened coming out of Nirvana with numb cheeks and a smile on my usually feisty face. Guru Steve hands me the staff to begin tonight's discussion. "Most of you remember Diane from our last retreat. Diane is a professor with expertise in Jungian psychology and the Enneagram, an ancient personality study."

Everyone just looks at me with blank stares. Expressions of emotion are not appropriate here. Clearly, I'm going to shake things up in no time.

"Diane, the topic today is: the day you were born. Talk between five and ten minutes and, when you're done, pass the staff to the person on the right."

"Thanks, Steve, and thanks to all of you for voting me into the group. Well, I'll make it short. My mother miscarried my twin brother at four months. I remained in the womb against a million-to-one odds. I was born a month early, with rosy cheeks and reddish brown hair. My doctor told my mother to raise me like a rare orchid because I might be delicate for the first few years of my life," I say with kind of a childlike voice.

The anesthesiologist across from me raises his hand, "We focus on absolute truth here. You could not have survived after your twin died," he says.

"Well, it is the only truth I know, sir."

Guru Steve motions me to pass the staff to the right. The sharing continues with mostly typical stories, but I have to admit Guru Steve's topic was a good one.

After our share time, we returned to our pillows for light yoga exercises: Downward Dog, Child's Pose, and finally, Shavasana.

Individual assignments were handed out before our closing, which was a cleansing ceremony with sage sticks. While a collection basket didn't exist, all of the attendees knew the ceramic bowl with Buddha on the side was meant for donations. I couldn't help noticing some of the checks were in the hundreds. I tossed a few bucks in and headed out the door.

The anesthesiologist follows me out, "Hey, I didn't mean to offend you. I guess the circumstances of your birth would vary according to the year you were born. I'm assuming that you are in your late forties, early fifties."

"So, did you say that shit earlier just to find out my age? You could have just asked me, but I guess that would be breaking one of Guru Steve's rules. I remember you now. You accused me of being a Diva in a card you put in my room at the beginning of the silent retreat."

"I wrote your assignment for this week. Guru Steve is training me to take over the group. Don't take it too personally. I'm just trying to help. You have potential."

Potential for what: to have sex with you, donate a large sum of money, or both? Guru Steve has to have his ducks in a row, but the good doctor is a bossy son of a bitch. I'll stay in the group for a while just to torture the pompous ass.

Assignment, Fall 2008: Make an attempt to avoid mirrors, give away five pieces of your favorite jewelry, and research the ancient figure Narcissus from Greek mythology.

Seriously, who does the anesthesiologist think he is? I'll ignore him. Guru Steve will only be attending a vipassana retreat on Maui for a week. Maybe I'll skip the group while Steve is gone. Actually, I may never go back. I probably got caught up in being invited to an exclusive group. Just being a Diva again.

27

Benny's

No one has ever called me "sweet" with the exception of Bruce, one of my professors, who is a gay man. Bruce sees through all of my ironclad mechanisms. We're tied together. Our complex relationship has been a natural progression of letting the business connection evolve into a personal bond.

I hear whistling before I actually see Bruce walking toward Benny's. His gate is heavy. Sensuality rolls off his broad shoulders. His eyes focus on his destination. Bruce looks approachable as he enters the restaurant in his black shorts, a black, short-sleeve shirt, and white running shoes. The hostess takes him by the arm and leads him to our booth.

Here he comes. I'll have him all to myself in a minute . . . but how could I really have someone like Bruce all to myself when he is loved by so many?

"How are you, honey?"

"Better, things are better," I lie.

Bruce has always filled in the emotional gaps that are missing in my marriage. Being with him tonight will help heal the wounds I'm dealing with after my last visit to New York. We both know Alex can't handle hearing about Veronica's suicide threat or Sam's brain tumor.

"Honey, you were attracted to Alex's bohemian way of life. He's so different from the statistician you married the first time. You didn't know that you married a man with Asperger's. After you got so busy making your fortune, you found ways to have a life separate from your marriage. Money isn't everything—health and happiness are more important."

"I have worked hard, Bruce. Another divorce would be devastating, not only for me, but also for my family. Did you see my new Series 3 BMW parked out front? My financial success has brought out the ambitious Diva in me. Trips to Paris every year, designer purses, plenty of good booze in the house. It beats being single and poor. Alex does the behind-the-scene parts of the company. He's a tech genius. I couldn't do DMC without him. Don't forget, Alex is also one of the top stained-glass artists in Denver."

Bruce reminds me Asperger's gets worse with age. He also challenges my Diva tendencies, claiming I really don't care about being rich. I feel exposed by the fact Bruce sees right through my pretentiousness.

"Look at this place, Bruce, it's such a dive with its flashing red and green lights and tequila ads all over the walls. The table is greasy, and look at the cuts on the leather seat. God help me if I have to pee. I never use the bathroom here."

"I know, but it's our place, honey. You love the turquoise door. Look at the fake roses on the table. Can you smell the chili pepper candle?" Bruce knows I can get testy when he exposes who I am under my Diva mask. He orders a Bud Light, a silver margarita straight up, salt and lime on the side, and a large guacamole … as if I didn't just act like a total bitch.

The voluptuous waitress bends over Bruce in her black, low-cut, Spanish-style dress.

After we finish the appetizer and the first round of drinks, I ask a question that has been burning in my throat for a long time. I slowly inhale and exhale deeply. My body starts to relax. "Bruce, what is this thing we have?" My legs are shaking under the table because I'm afraid I'm making a complete fool out of myself.

Bruce starts singing along with the music in the background. I think singing will help me calm down, so I join in.

"Another one bites the dust … don't you love Queen? I saw them at Red Rocks. Why does our relationship have to have words? Sometimes words get in the way."

"I'm falling in love with you, Bruce. I feel so vulnerable right now. You're the one who shares your feelings, while I'm the tough girl looking for a good time, most nights." I've nearly drained my second margarita.

"Right. Tough on the outside, but I see under all that crap. You're a softy! Look at what you've done for others in your lifetime. You don't run around telling people your family was totally messed up. Your only advocate, Pop, sexually abused you, for God's sake. How about Veronica threatening suicide recently?"

Bruce is right. My mother has the right mix of inner demons to be considered textbook crazy. I still have my third grade report card to document the fact she kept me home from school for forty days that year when I was rarely actually sick. Today, social services would be investigating her. I feel my neck turn red as I watch a diamond-shaped tear fall onto Bruce's cheek. I rarely cry because I'm afraid if I do, I won't be able to stop.

"What about you, Bruce? Oh my God, your father, a minister, brought his mistress into your family home. In spite of everything he did, you took care of him when he was dying. You almost went bankrupt doing so."

"You know that all too well. You saved me from losing everything. Don't ever be hard on yourself in front of me. You're like an Oreo cookie: two pieces of chocolate cookie with sweet, creamy icing in the middle."

I'm so turned on, I use a menu to fan myself. I'm afraid I might try to make out with Bruce in some dark corner outside the restaurant. Bruce and I are having an emotional affair, which can be more intense than a sexual affair. I decide it's time to jump into our business relationship.

"Honey, remember when we talked about driving to Taos to take a memoir class? Now you're applying to the Book Project to write one! Success is a hungry tiger, honey. Take it slow."

"I still want to go to Taos with you, Bruce. We could develop a writing class together. How do you like 'Rose,' the scene I wrote in Vegas? Thanks for editing the piece. I love the way Rose, the cigarette girl, begins with a bunch of hawkers dressed in checkered suits standing outside the Flamingo Hotel, claiming to have the best deals on everything from a buffet at the Bellagio and Le Reve at the Wynn. Thanks, Bruce!"

I begin to read:

Bright, seductive slot machines click on at the Flamingo Hotel. I am drawn to the gentleman who's betting and talking on his cell phone. Is he a professional, betting for someone else? Is he a gangster? I can't help but be curious. Vegas is my favorite place for observing and developing characters. After I make a few notes about the gambler, a young cigarette girl catches my eye. Seriously, I can't remember the last time I saw a cigarette girl. I name her Rose. She's standing under a pink chandelier, selling roses and cigarettes. Rose is wearing a black bodysuit. Her black and red headband with black and pink bunny ears sit atop her long, black hair. Her black eyeliner and pomegranate-red lipstick seem out of sync with her childlike innocence.

"Miss, can I buy you a drink?" a man asks. "I just won big at the craps table. You can have anything you want."

"Bless your little heart, I don't drink, sir."

The man couldn't pass a breathalyzer test if his life depended on it. I want to make sure Rose can hold her own against a potential predator.

"May I have a rose, please?"

Rose hands me the biggest one in the bunch, a bright red one to match my lips. Her smile is so genuine it makes me want to pack up her display, get her a nice meal, and give her a couple thousand dollars.

"Hey, I'm doing business with the lady," the drunk says as he sneers at me, "but she's not really a lady, is she?"

The drunk upsets Rose's tray. Red roses and packs of cigarettes fly in every direction. I watch his hands move in circles on Rose's exposed belly. She signals security, but as soon as it looks like he's ready to move on, security backs off. I suppose they want to keep things calm in this popular casino.

I watch the drunk get in line to ride the Ferris wheel in front of the Flamingo.

"I hope you pass out at the top and crap your pants," I shout.

"Bitch!"

Pop used to pass out on the Ferris wheel in Palisades Park. I didn't tell Veronica that Pop was drunk every time we went because she would just tell me that at least I had a roof over my head.

"Honey," Bruce says, "I like your voice in the memoir more than I did in the mystery. Just take care of yourself. Bringing up the past can be hard on the body, and keep away from that vipassana group. You know how to meditate, and writing is really your best meditation. Just keep writing."

28

The Bartender

Researchers claim we have some 60,000 thoughts a day. My thoughts are all over the place today: is Bruce right, should I divorce Alex? Would I be able to feed my Diva lifestyle after a brutal divorce settlement? Can I develop a life of my own that will be satisfying instead of getting a divorce? As I walk around my neighborhood tonight, I realize that, while I have always been a Diva, freedom is more important to me now. No matter what happens, I will not only survive, I will thrive.

Great, I'm just in time for happy hour at the restaurant where I used to meet my blind dates in the mid-nineties. In fact, I had my first date with Alex here at the Park Grill.

"Good to see you again, Diane! Would you like a table or the bar tonight?" the hostess asks.

I take the last seat at the bar next to a tall, attractive man. He's wearing Titanium Revitalize pants and a Titanium Performance yoga tee. Looks like he's sipping a glass of something bubbly. A Perrier? The cougar next to him is all over him. From their conversation, I conclude he's a writer, and his name is Scott.

One of the cougars at the bar asks, "Are you always that seductive when you address an audience of intellectuals?" The woman giggles. "Seriously, I have never seen that many women standing in line to shake hands with a speaker at DU."

I notice Scott never loses eye contact with his giddy devotee, who would obviously go home with him tonight if he asked. He doesn't judge her obviously inebriated state; he simply doesn't say much. The woman mentions something about writing vignettes for an audience of "bad girls" who like soft porn.

Scott returns her obvious come-on with, "You should write what you want to write. No judgement here. Hey, I have to head back to Boulder soon. I'm finishing up a book proposal for a client. Have a great rest of your evening."

The cougar pays for Scott's drink and stumbles toward the door. She looks back at him one more time, but he doesn't budge from his seat until after she leaves.

"Does she come here often?" Scott asks the bartender.

"This bar and many more, I suspect. The thing is, the woman is filthy rich but just can't find happiness."

I continue to lick the sugar off my Cosmopolitan as I listen to him tell Scott about how he's a therapist as much as a mixologist. "You could write an article about bartenders. I'll be your first interview," he says.

Scott takes down a few notes, acting like he might do an interview in the future.

"Okay, so let me get this straight," Scott says, "You greet a single woman with a smile, protect all of her secrets, and craft the cocktail of her dreams. After a while, she realizes what she pays you pales in comparison to what she pays a therapist. Keeps the ladies coming back, right?" Scott congratulates him for having the perfect job.

The bartender laughs so hard he has to apologize to everyone at the bar.

When a friend from my writing group stops by to share some writing, Scott hands her a business card. "Would you like one too? Diane, isn't it? Keep writing, ladies. Have a nice evening."

I finish the evening in the park, hoping to walk off my two Cosmos on the way to the boathouse. It looks so romantic. There's a thin layer of ice on the lake that makes the water look like it's covered with diamonds. I make three wishes and throw a piece of driftwood into the water.

Later, I tuck Scott's business card into my turquoise Tiffany box that sits in my nightstand along with my stack of journals, violet lip gloss, and expensive night creams. There's vodka on my breath as I focus on my breathing. I am too high to go downstairs for my yoga mat. Instead, I grab a large, blue silk pillow from my reading chair. I sit in front of one of my favorite paintings of a figure that looks like Marilyn Monroe, another Diva like me. "Let thoughts pass by without judgement," I remember from vipassana meditation. My cheeks are starting to feel numb before I leave the lotus position.

I can't keep myself from calling him. "Hi Scott, this is Diane Morrison, we met last night at Park Grill. I'm in the beginning stages of looking for a writing coach. According to your website, you offer a thirty-minute complimentary session to explain your style. I look forward to hearing from you."

When Scott returns my call, I know after fifteen minutes he prefers writers who are working on a memoir. When he asks for twenty pages of my writing, I admit I wrote a scene that could be part of a memoir and fifteen pages of a mystery I started six months ago. The remarks Scott sends back on the mystery are: *nice sentences, but I love the nonfiction piece, "Rose."*

Scott is intelligent, well read, honest, and a no-nonsense kind of coach. Working with him would be much harder than going to my writing group where only positive remarks are allowed. Scott is definitely not going to kiss my ass, in fact, he will probably kick my ass.

Our first phone session goes like this, "You sent me a shit load of words, Diane. Are you serious about writing? If the answer is yes, do you want to publish? I'm leaving soon to spend three weeks in India. Would you like to set up another session before I leave?"

My answer is certainly not based on Scott's charm, but on recommendations from several employees at the Boulder Book Store who know him. I convince myself he'll be warmer when he gets back from three weeks of hanging out with gurus in India. He can be a little rough around the edges. The truth is, I love Scott's voice and his rugged attitude about life. I figure I can still work on the mystery, go to my writing group, and work with Scott at the same time. This, however, quickly proves impossible.

Scott's first two sessions are over my head, to be honest. He loses patience with me during our third phone session because he's leaving for India in two days and had been in a car accident earlier that day. A woman banged into his new Kia Soul in the Trader Joe's parking lot while mindlessly backing out of her parking space. She nonchalantly mentioned her back-up camera was dirty.

"I would have asked the bitch why she didn't turn her head before she pulled out," he said, but quickly turned his focus back to me. "It's okay, Diane, let's focus on your writing. Here it is: every memoir needs conflict, empathy, and suspense. Give me obstacles that last long enough to get me hooked. I want a page-turner from you, but don't spill the beans too fast.

Write and then wait. Make the reader crave an outcome. Get inside the reader's head."

I wonder if he makes love this way. I think I will pay for more sessions soon, forgetting I'm married and Scott has a girlfriend. While Scott is in India, I focus on an upcoming benefit for the Denver Art Museum—a catered event in our home.

29

Denver Art Museum

Alex is quite a mixologist! Tonight he plans a concoction with gin, Champagne, and fresh grapefruit juice. I enjoy watching him put his ingredients together in the Ralph Lauren shaker I gave him for his birthday. Although we're completely opposite in temperament, I look at him, and he looks at me. There's a bond between us—between Alex's left-brain introversion and my extroverted, right-brain personality. I call him the Buddha; he calls me the Diva.

Art is the glue that holds our marriage together. Tonight we're talking about where to hang our newest painting, by San Francisco artist, Mann. The most important thing with any acquisition is finding the best light source for the work.

The Mann painting, a romantic portrait of a Russian woman, ends up in a niche under a large spotlight. The model is an illusion of a woman with long, blonde hair adorned with white feathers and a single pink rose. *Jillian* appears to be sitting on a cloud of wispy, white paint, tinted with subtle, gray-green brush strokes. Her cream, satin robe with ecru lace is open to her waist, exposing her youthful breasts. This thirty-six by twenty-four-inch painting in an ornate silver frame is a showstopper in our collection.

While hanging the piece, Alex quotes from Saint Thomas Aquinas: "Stay near beauty, for she will always strengthen you."

One never knows what the public will admire the most when viewing an art collection like ours. The group sponsoring the event mentions beforehand the attendees will want to see our French gardens as well as the paintings. The perennials look good, the roses have been pruned, and the annuals are blooming nicely.

Damn it, I know that sound! It's a downpour, and I'm sure it will be followed by hail. Alex runs to the garage to grab our collection of plant covers as I store the chaise lounge cushions in the basement. Loud sirens warn us we need to take cover in the basement. Tornadoes sometimes hit along with hail.

"Alex, we need to go downstairs now!" I yell.

"Just let me cover the last few roses. It isn't going to be that bad, babe, the hail is only pea-sized."

He's soaking wet, clothes sticking to him, by the time he joins me in the basement. Thick towels and a shot of whiskey take his mind off the hail for a few minutes. We watch lumps of ice hit the well cover, and some of the pieces bounce off violently and hit the shrubs behind the well.

"Think about chunks of ice hitting the roof. There could be roof damage, babe."

"Geeze, didn't we replace the roof a couple of years ago?"

When the hail stops, we go outside. The yard looks like a disaster with tree branches strewn all over, roses stripped of petals, small plants pummeled, and ice piled up everywhere.

The weatherman asks at 5 p.m., "Is it springtime or the night before Christmas?"

Alex spends most of the afternoon shoveling hail off the sidewalk and the front courtyard while I work on getting rid of droopy flowers and dead leaves. The next morning, we're the first customers at the closest garden center.

Although the gardens are still a mess, we're confident those who paid for the museum event will focus more on our paintings. We can afford to buy what the experts call *master artists*. Since the museum only features one collector a year, this is quite an honor for Alex and me.

By the time people arrive for the event, there are just a few signs of the hailstorm remaining, including a small bump on Alex's head. He'd stayed out in the hail too long.

The guests arrive in stages. I'm the first tour guide. Alex follows me with the second group. We take the museum hosts and two groups of collectors all through our house. When the tours end and the refreshments have been served, those who remain gather in the living room to ask questions about our collection.

When asked why we collect art, Alex says, "Those who create are close to the creator, the universal genius. It's a spiritual experience for me."

"I'm addicted to beauty, and collecting art is my latest addiction," I add.

One of the attendees assures me that a love of beauty isn't a bad addiction. I wish Veronica was alive to hear the remark because, in a sense, she too was addicted to beauty. Toward the end of her life, Veronica did watercolor painting. I suspected her years in assisted living were happy. The hospital staff nicknamed her Mother Teresa because she became saintly before she died.

"From a practical standpoint," Alex continues, "Diane and I consider our collection to be a legacy for future generations."

"Collecting art as an investment might be higher risk than investing in the stock market, but it's undeniably more pleasurable," I add.

A woman who looks like a piece of art herself asks if we ever get too attached to a particular artist.

"Well, yes of course. Alex and I travel all over the world to attend openings for our favorite artists. We have several pieces of Mann's work in our collection. We flew to San Francisco for his one-man show at John Pence Gallery earlier this year, and we are flying to Santa Fe next month for what Mann claims will be his last show for a while. He wants to make films."

People get a kick out of our stories about Nicholas Martin, a French artist who stayed with us last year. Thinking that Nico, a strikingly handsome man with a shaved head and clear blue eyes, would want French food, we made an effort to serve a typical *petit dejeuner*. We bought pastries, baguettes, and special coffees. It turned out that Nico preferred a sugar cookie, a Red Bull, and a cigarette for breakfast.

"Our home is open to artists and gallery owners. Our son, Craig, calls me the Gertrude Stein of Denver. Well sure, I am a true patron, and I love to wear my party clothes, flaunt my Diva style, and even put on a performance."

When one of the collectors asks if I would be willing to sell her one of our small, still life paintings, I delay my answer for two days. In the meantime, the woman offers us twice the price agreed on earlier. We accept her offer.

The two-day event raises two thousand dollars for the Denver Art Museum. Some attendees give donations in addition to the price of a ticket, and the painting we sell from our collection ends up paying for our stay in Santa Fe.

As Alex and I fly into Santa Fe, I wonder what I will learn in such a diverse town. The combination of Catholics, Sikhs, Hindus, and Native

Americans gives an ephemeral energy that heals me. Alex and I spend the first day on the plaza taking in the sights, sounds, and smells of downtown. There are several charming beggars who offer to hypnotize me, uncover past lives, and give me essential oils. I put a small amount of the essential oils on my wrists after having a margarita infused with burnt sage. Night falls, but I don't notice because I'm caught up in reading my pocket journal full of notes about people I meet.

Cafe Rosita's inspires my design sense the next morning. The walls are covered with colorful Mexican tiles and strings of red, white, and green flags strung across the dining room.

"Are you trying to figure out everyone's personality types at the table?" Alex asks.

"Not yet. Did you get shots of the Mexican tiles and the flags?"

I can't resist buying one of everything from a street vendor who sells paper flowers, beaded bracelets, and packages of Mexican hard candies in Cafe Rosita's. I reach out to touch the woman's weathered hand because she reminds me of pictures I've seen of Mexican saints.

Before moving to another table, the woman tells me to take a medal of Saint Michael because Addie told her I will need his protection in the near future.

Addie was very eccentric. Her psychedelic style, bright cotton dresses, and rainbow-dyed hair defined her gypsy personality. It would be just like her to send a gypsy with a religious medal my way.

"You remind me of Addie when you dress like a gypsy, babe."

"True, I do have some of her gypsy side, but Addie was never a Diva like me. She raised seven of her siblings and then six kids. Addie never had the time or the money to be pretentious like me."

Mann's elegant opening is just the occasion for my long, black, belted dress, meant to accentuate the triple layers of turquoise necklaces around my neck. My black and turquoise cowboy boots add to the Southwestern look.

Alex and I have a scintillating conversation with Mann, who is typically shy. My words sound trite compared to what the artist has to say tonight. Mann admits he started his artistic journey to understand not only himself, but the world around him.

Mann holds my hands as if he has known me for a long time. "Avoid those who keep you from evolving. Follow your dreams of painting and writing. Love life and all the shit in it. Invest in yourself. Doing art is the only way to get better at it. Every creation trains not only your skills, but opens your eyes to new ways of solving problems," he says.

When we return to Denver, Mann's pieces are more precious to me than they were before. I simply need to be with one of his paintings.

"You've been standing by *Jillian* for almost an hour."

"I know, Alex."

30

Living Out Loud

I need a massage to clear the residue of a boozy trip to Santa Fe. My body can't shake off the spicy food and tequila fast enough. Sophia, a Rolfer and former dancer, is tall, with perfect posture. I watch her check my body alignment before she asks about what's going on in my life.

"How are you doing, Diane?"

"Well, I feel as if I'm living the good life, Sophia. Traveling the world, painting, collecting art, starting a memoir, and my company continues to flourish."

"Great, do you have specific questions before I start the massage?"

"Let me know if you pick up on anything about my writing coach, Scott. It's probably a matter of transference and countertransference, but is there more going on between us?"

Sophia leaves the room and I remove my purple boots and strip down. I stretch out under the sheets face down on the table. After thirty minutes of working on my upper back, Sophia goes lower and deeper.

"Have you been drinking a lot lately? Your liver area is off."

"I just got back from Santa Fe. You know I party hard when I travel. Yes, I drank too much there."

"Increase your vitamin D3. You need to clear physical and psychological toxins. Tell me, what precautions are you taking while you work on your memoir? Are you meditating before you write and after your memories surface? Some memoir writers have suffered physical illness and even mental breakdowns while writing about the past."

Sophia finishes our time together with a meditation. I feel healing energy extend from her to me, leaving me with something similar to hands-on prayer, although her hands are not actually touching me. "Diane, my guides are telling me you and Scott are twin flames. He's not someone you met in a former life. You essentially have the same soul. Both parts of this soul have come back together to fulfill a special purpose in this lifetime."

"Is it possible Scott is my twin brother who was miscarried at four months? That idea sounds more reasonable to me, Sophia."

"My guides say no, you have the same soul. When twin flames succeed in making a connection, one twin is the chaser, the other is the runner. Obviously you are the runner . . . you look petrified right now!"

This information is way over my head. I just wanted to know if Scott and I are going to end up having an affair. Sophia's bodywork continues without words until I ask her if I should find a different writing coach.

"Meditate before you make any decisions about Scott. You two need to meet in public places. Your chemistry is very strong. He does understand your Diva style, which is a benefit to your writing."

Sophia sends me home with a vial of essential oils to balance my past-life connections with Scott. My attraction to him remains underground, like the tiny root of a walnut tree: one that is not visible, but I know it's there. I'm much too busy to deal with this craziness. It sounds like I'm just falling in love with myself.

Time passes. I keep writing, and Scott keeps coaching. We meet twice a month in a hotel lobby in Boulder. He greets me with a warm smile, and I greet him with a small gift. Today his gift is a pomegranate. I watch him pull out the seeds of what he tells me is his favorite fruit.

"The pomegranate is a symbol of temptation. According to an old myth, Aphrodite, the goddess of love, planted the first pomegranate tree," he says.

"Good to know, my muse, I will never look at a pomegranate the same way again."

This is the beginning of my understanding a good writer either literally knows everything or can convince you he does. Scott obviously reads and does research on many subjects.

"Listen, you need to step up the amount of words you're writing. I'm going to start cracking the whip."

Is this the way he typically warms up before a session?

"I like whips," I say.

"So do I," he says, with a perfunctory nod.

As time passes, I catch a glimpse of where Scott is taking me. I expect a long journey of self-discovery and the uncovering of what he calls my "evocative writing powers."

When I tell him I'm physically attracted to him, he teaches me about *agape love*. "*Agape* derives from the Ancient Greek for *godly love*. *Gape* also means an expression of wonder that we may not have words to describe. *Agape* is hard to see because we all have screens. My screens are papers with words on them," Scott says.

"My screen is the Diva mask I wear to avoid feeling pain. Are you telling me I should think about divine love to avoid the pain of the terrible possibility of falling in love?"

"We'll see."

Working with Scott gives me a new sense of acceptance, much deeper than self-esteem. After looking at my entire life, all the good and bad pieces, it scares me to be unconditional with myself because it makes me feel vulnerable. I'm letting down my guard. I might get hurt, but I know if that happens, my warrior side will come out. Divas are much more than showpieces.

Scott reminds me I may feel uncentered for a while and will eventually come back to feeling comfortable again. The writing, he claims, will activate this journey of discovering my authentic self.

"What you have on the page is like a da Vinci drawing of something the artist is going to paint later. I'm talking about the guts of the words that need to be arranged in such a way that the reader will be able to embrace your Diva-ness."

When I look in the mirror the following day, March 17, 2019, almost forty years after I had a mastectomy, I realize it really doesn't matter whether we are seven or seventy-seven, we are still the same beings at any age—yet American culture seems to consider women over sixty to be invisible. An awareness of invisibility will not shape my decisions in the future. I'm a fearless risk-taker. Some women are not meant to be tame at any age. I'm like a coyote: indestructible!

I awaken alone in the Blue Room and feel as if I have slept for a long time. My consciousness is deepening. I feel light-headed, yet full of energy, and completely aware of who I am and what I need to do to nurture myself.

When I tell Scott I experienced a type of ecstasy, he says, "You felt *agape* love, a deep, primitive source of love. You actually *became* love, Diane."

31

Premonition

I fax Scott before I leave Denver for my next session with him. Encountering less traffic from Denver to Boulder allows me to drive up Boulder Canyon because I have an extra thirty minutes to kill before our meeting. My favorite Coldplay CD plays as I take in the fields of fall foliage.

I follow the edge of the oak woods, stopping to pick up a curious little pine branch, thinking I will use it and its needles to add texture to a Jackson Pollock style painting I'm working on. I use a different branch to tap the undergrowth of several oak trees, wanting to touch the saplings underneath. One appears to be surviving well. I mark it with a ribbon that was tied around my journal. My focus remains on the oak forest, as if I knew then that this forest would be my refuge in troubled times ahead. I would return to this spot many times during the COVID-19 pandemic . . . but everything was still perfect that day in late November. How could I or anyone know the earth and its people would be turned upside down less than a year later?

Scott is running late, which gives me time to check out a new machine in the hotel lobby: Zoltar, a nostalgic fortune teller automaton who sits in front of a blue satin curtain. He's wearing a gold satin shirt with a black tapestry vest. There's also a red turban with a gold, bejeweled band around his latex head.

"I am Zoltar, come on over," he says, his eyes moving from side to side. "For a small fee I can predict your future. Your future is mine for the telling and yours for the knowing. Zoltar speaks." The repetition of this machine inspires me to do a quick write on a piece of scrap paper. The white noise of his voice, repeating the same thing over and over, keeps my pen moving.

When Scott arrives, we align our computers and nibble on French pastries. Scott adds two Americanos to the table. We're set to begin. Scott starts.

"I teach you about storytelling. Unlike my other writers, you take what I give you and make the writing yours. The psychic chapter has a strong voice. You're questioning yourself and the psychic at the same time. I would like you to write more about your concept of love as you move through the next few chapters. It didn't land on me until today—you consider falling in love to be spiritual. You connect with the depth of the universe by falling in love."

"You're right, Scott. I'm in love. I can't wait to be with the object of my love. I want to hear his voice, touch him, grab the beads around his neck. What I feel reminds me of something Steve Jobs expressed right before he died. He said 'Wow!' over and over until his last breath. I never want to compromise falling in love. Falling in love is my 'Wow!'"

"You can be in love with more than one person because different people show you different parts of yourself. Think about it—what I'm saying lines up with Jungian psychology. The question is: are you falling in love with a person, with yourself, or are you simply falling in love with love, Diane?"

One of us is missing the point here. I'm falling in love with Scott, who's twenty-four years younger than me and a year younger than Craig.

As if Scott can read my mind he says, "Baby, you look great for your age!"

Now more than ever, I decide to never hold back on love again, but I feel vulnerable, maybe anxious. Life is never easy, and I sense it's never going to be easier. In the midst of trying my best to create a life, my soul tells me I must, while this chemistry with Scott screams out at me.

"Okay, you are a million miles away right now. What do you think about going back to the beginning of your memoir when we see how you became a Diva, not just the Shirley Temple stuff. Yes, you were a performer, even a character. I want to know more about your pretentiousness. I see you in an actor's dressing room, taking your makeup off metaphorically. Use the Blue Room for your contemplative thinking to explore your authentic self."

"Okay, Scott, then I'll see you again in about a year! It will take me a year or more."

"Yeah, writing a memoir is a gift and a curse!" He flashes his signature cheeky smile.

When my coach leaves, I go back to Zoltar. A fortune, printed on canary-yellow paper with black astrological signs around the edges, pops out immediately. I see a great deal of happiness in store for you. Happiness never decreases when shared. Most of our pleasures come from unexpected sources. Share the good news when it comes. Zoltar speaks.

The astrological signs on Zoltar's fortune remind me of the first time I met with Dora. I gaze at the astrological signs on Zoltar's fortune, remembering how my psychic used small plastic figures: an archer for Sagittarius, my sun sign, and the twins for Gemini, my moon sign. My astrology chart had helped her access some of my personality traits. After several appointments with her in her eccentric office in Boulder or her beautiful home in Boulder Canyon, Dora helped me sharpen my gifts and accept my pretentiousness. Pretentiousness is what we do every day. It keeps life interesting.

I remember Oscar Wilde: "Man is least himself when he talks in his own person. Give him a mask, and he will tell you the truth."

32

Pretentious

I'm going back in time to access my baby self, the little darling known as Cookie, a nickname my father gave me which stuck until I married Anthony. I'm sure Pop wanted me to be a sweetie, but the moniker also brought other disgusting labels such as Cutie, Darlin', Hon, and Pussy in my teens. These descriptors just don't fit me . . . well, maybe Pussy!

Where the hell is my baby book? I'm not sure if I unpacked it after the renovation in 2008. There it is—underneath my box of Prada heels in the Blue Room closet.

I open the pink satin book and a neatly-folded parchment paper falls at my feet.

November 24, 1942

Dearest Angel and Cookie,

Oh Angel, Cookie's birth a month earlier than your due date comes as such a surprise to me! I'm still in a whirl! I feel so bad, my dear, that you had to go through all this alone. Oh, you are such a little heroine.

I'm so happy it's a baby girl, and I hear she has your beautiful features. My Cookie made me the proudest Daddy in the whole wide world.

I mailed Pop my phone number this morning. You can call me, dear, when you feel strong enough. Try me in the evenings. I keep to myself when the boys go out to drink. Remember, I am always faithful to you, dear. I love you so much, so much!

Your faithful hubby,

Bob

XXX Angel

X Cookie

P.S. The Major has agreed to give me a furlough in a couple of weeks, Veronica. I am glad because there are rumors we may be sent overseas soon, dear.

My Father saw me once before he was commissioned to serve in Europe. I have one photograph of him holding me in a movie theater, of all places. Robert's furlough from his base in North Carolina was the last time he saw me.

I'm sure friends and family spoiled me rotten because of the war and because of the fact my father was so well-loved. When Robert was killed in Aachen, Germany, two and a half years later, things got worse. Veronica began dressing me in designer clothes. Many years later, my therapist said I was more of a doll than a child to her. Veronica wrote things in the baby book about how often people would stop her on the street just to take a picture of me. I graduated from just being cute and sweet to being a little Diva.

These facts, plus the show-off I became when I performed for my Jersey City family, guaranteed me a pretentious style.

In his book *Pretentiousness: Why It Matters*, Dan Fox mentions, "In politics, the claimant to a throne or similar rank was called a pretender. To be called a 'pretender' was not necessarily an insult." In my case, being a pretender not only protected me as a child, but also made me successful as an adult. No one calls me "Sweet Cookie" now. "Tough Cookie" is a much better way to describe me. It was actually my Aunt Iris who named me Tough Cookie.

She never saw me as the war hero's daughter who had to be pampered and kept home for the slightest sniffle.

We all wear metaphorical masks, especially when we are unwilling to show the parts of ourselves we prefer to keep hidden. Carl Jung referred to our hidden parts as our *shadows*. I know I work hard to keep my shadow under wraps when I'm speaking to an audience. I never want a group of teachers to know I'm nervous or making stuff up to keep their attention. I keep these educators engaged because I'm on fire, strutting my pretentiousness. I'm not really a guru, but they think I am. When they give me standing ovations, I take a bow.

Pretentiousness lines up with being a Diva. I'm sassy and savvy. I never make excuses for my irreverence or my brassy New York style of speaking. I am not the kind of Diva who gets upset if she doesn't get the newest Louis Vuitton cross-body purse in Amarante. Glamor is important to me, but having grit and being true to myself are more important.

Like my Aunt Iris, I know how to use being a Diva to become well known. Iris started to design elegant lingerie in 1938 and became internationally famous in war time. Over the years, Iris won awards for her designs. It's my aunt's strength I want to emulate. It must have been a challenge to be a Jewish woman selling lingerie in Europe during World War II. Her seductive toga nightdress caused fashion critics of the time to credit her for making a nightgown elegant enough to wear in public. Women were photographed wearing Iris lingerie under their mink coats. When Christian Dior made trips to NYC, he visited Iris Designs to stock up on lingerie for models in Paris. Givenchy did the same. Iris's international fame was set in stone.

The Metropolitan Museum has a collection of Iris Designs, including my favorite nightdress—part of her Pretty Little Girls series—described as having a "sweet length, soft lace, and dreams of yesteryear." I admit this design is very different from her other more pretentious gowns from the fifties and sixties, but I love it because I had a nightgown from my aunt's Little Girls series.

Looking at a display of Iris's pieces from the late sixties at the Met makes me want to get past the museum guard to stand next to my aunt's display. I would love to take this opportunity to applaud her and anyone else who braves stepping outside the norm of our culture.

I can't help noticing a woman watching me as we both stand in front of the collection of Iris Lingerie. "Excuse me," she says. "You are wearing a gold headband like one that Iris wore just before she died. She became more flamboyant in her later years. Did you know her?"

"She was my aunt."

"I'm Estelle, I was one of Iris's seamstresses. Do you want me to take a photo of you in front of Iris's display? I saw you slip off your shoes. Were you thinking of climbing up on the display? Iris would have gotten a kick out of your chutzpah, but the guard is watching you like a hawk. Good luck to you. Cookie, is it? Actually, Iris called you a Tough Cookie, and a Cheeky Diva. She told me you did interesting sketches of costumes when you were young. She wondered if you would become an actress."

"Actually, I'm Diane, Estelle. It's wonderful to meet you. Can I buy you a cup of tea or a glass of Champagne? I know very little about Aunt Iris because I was kept away from my father's side of the family."

Estelle stayed in the museum long enough to meet Alex. She scurried off to attend an evening of poetry reading in a small chapel close to the Met. I gave her one of my business cards.

"Estelle is a beautiful woman. I enjoy seeing an older woman in vintage clothing. You would look great in a vintage hat like hers," Alex smiles.

"One of my favorite vintage hat stores is on 5th Avenue. We will both get something. Aunt Iris would have loved the idea."

It took me a year to be honest with myself about why Tough Cookie is still one of my monikers after so many years. I'm guessing Iris knew my early childhood was far from being normal. Many people still call me Tough Cookie. It's true: I will do anything to get what I want. Some say I can be difficult to deal with, especially the professors who are part of my consulting company.

Being tough doesn't mean I'm unemotional, but I rarely cry. In fact, I sometimes laugh when I'm sad. My shell is hard, but my insides are soft. My friend Bruce had it right when he called me an Oreo Cookie—hard on the outside, soft on the inside.

God help me, Aunt Iris was right on with the Cheeky Diva moniker. I'm sure if she were still alive she would delight in my pretentiousness.

33

London, 2020

Am I being foolish when I decide to go to London at the beginning of the pandemic, a year after my last visit to the Metropolitan Museum? I consciously avoid learning anything about the virus before I leave to visit my granddaughter Zoe in Kensington. Is it pretentious of me to think everything will be fine this visit? I could pretend I am going back in time before people started dying from a virus even the scientists were then scratching their heads about.

The Uber driver in London, wearing a mask, holds a sign that reads "Diane Morrison" in perfect block letters. He stands with formal posture at Heathrow Airport.

My twenty-five-percent-British heritage feels more like fifty percent as I naturally absorb the formality of how the Brits assist travelers with the utmost politeness. Since I have a natural tendency to take on different accents, I sound less American the more I speak. To be honest, I even learned a few Cockney words in case I need them at pubs: *ta ta* for goodbye, *cheeky* for sexy, *turtle dove* for love, and *in the sink* for drunk.

Thank God the Uber driver is talkative because the drive from Heathrow to Bloomsbury is over an hour long. Many of the streets ordinarily open are blocked today. The mayor of London wants more bike trails around the city, which may be very proactive, but London streets are narrow and the bikes make it hard for vehicles, especially tour buses, to navigate.

"What is it like living in London, sir? Do you miss your native country?" I ask to break the awkward silence in the van.

"Living in London is challenging, but I'm very happy to be here instead of in Ukraine. My wife and I live in an apartment with one bedroom. We have two young children, so we gave up part of our kitchen to make a small bedroom for them."

"Kurva blyat!" he yells at a driver who is on the wrong side of the street. "My apologies, madam. Sorry I dropped the F-bomb."

The possibility of having an accident with a car driving on the wrong side of the street, brought back a memory of a similar accident: the last time I was in England the summer of 1986.

"Oh my God, oh my God!" I yelled. "You're on the wrong side of the road, Anthony."

Before my husband could move to the correct side of the road, we were hit head-on by a young man and his girlfriend. They hit the windshield and rolled off the top of the car, ending up on a grassy field.

Someone in the pub we just left in the Cotswolds, which are outside of London, called an ambulance. My son, Craig, and my daughter, Michelle, have never forgotten that the cops let their inebriated father walk away without as much as a ticket for an accident that was his fault. Apparently the cops preferred tourists to young, heavy-metal locals.

After a trip to the emergency room to get glass taken out of my forehead, three of us wanted to check on the victims, but Anthony ruled that out. He walked away from what he did, and the rest of us have never forgotten his inability to be wrong. My body cringed when he tried to put his arm around me before we left the hospital, and my kids, especially Michelle, were upset the rest of the trip. I knew then my marriage was going to be hard to mend.

Some personalities are just harder to bridge. Anthony's critical nature was holding me, an adventurer, back. A good relationship allows each person to grow and flourish. We did not have a good relationship. It ended eight years after my first trip to London.

Alex nudges me because the driver is asking if we have collected any Russian artists. Alex, an introvert, must have told the driver we collect art. I love it when my husband prefers to do the talking. I quickly mention an artist couple who do egg tempera paintings together. I see a text from my son. Craig is checking on our arrival in London. He wonders if we have contacted Zoe yet. I too am wondering how Zoe is surviving in London. She is studying here and is dealing with the challenges of living in a big city. Her home is in suburban southern California. Two days ago she had her phone, cash, credit card, and ID stolen at a Starbucks in Kensington. It was probably a set-up between one of the brewsters and the thief. No one stepped up to help her, poor girl. She was one of a few Americans in the cafe.

Zoe was in tears when we met her at the train station the day of our arrival. She cried when we handed her an iPhone, credit card, and cash.

When Alex and I arrive at the Empress at the Gardens on February 27, 2020, there's a group of Hasidic Jews praying in the lobby. We walk past them in their black face masks, white robes, tasseled prayer shawls, and big black hats. I must admit, their chanting is soothing until I hear the rabbi say the word "pandemic," followed by a litany of prayers in Hebrew.

There aren't any confirmed cases of the virus in London when we arrive. By the time we store our bags, the men have gone on to warn others that "the end of days are here."

With that unsettling message in mind, Alex and I walk around Bloomsbury, checking out the Irish wool shops until our room is ready. London is damp and cold this time of year. We stock up on scarves, hats, and heavy socks appropriate for my Diva style—meaning the total will be expensive. As I watch my warm clothing go into shopping bags, I am reminded of the time Alex took me to NYC in the middle of January. "Remember I had to buy a ridiculously expensive coat, a gigantic wool scarf to cover my face, and sheepskin-lined mittens when we met Rick and Trish at a bed and breakfast by Columbia a year after the millennium, Alex?"

"Yes, and I also remember it cost a fortune in cab fare because you complained the cold air was making your face hurt and all the expensive face cream wouldn't make up for the cold air damage."

I wonder if the Londoners will think my need for excessive woolen clothes is a bunch of malarkey. The locals walk around with very little outer clothing, claiming they condition their bodies to be comfortable in cold weather.

The cashier hands Alex my shopping bag and turns to me. "Are you that American actress who was in *Thelma & Louise*, miss? We get some famous actresses in our shop, they usually need more than their fur coats to protect their lily-soft skin in this bitter cold."

I want to have a little fun with her before I leave by pretending to be Susan Sarandon, but I just nod, leaving it up to her to decide if I am, in fact, Thelma. She happily adds an Aran wool sweater and a flask with an embossed Celtic cross to a second shopping bag which she hands to me.

"Where can I get a good bottle of Irish whiskey? This Nordic air is getting to me."

"Believe it or not, there's a small liquor store in the basement of the Italian restaurant across the street. You can have a nice lunch there. Be sure to check out the Lotus Heart Bookstore as well."

When Alex tells me the Brits are into various types of metaphysics, especially tarot, going to Lotus Heart Bookstore is our plan after lunch.

The store, with a whole section of books on fairies and leprechauns, makes me think about Addie, who loved to cast an innocent spell on sanctimonious priests now and then. Addie wore a tree of life necklace, like one in the jewelry case, which protected her from evil spirits and guaranteed her a long life, she claimed.

Gertrude, the owner, tells us about the tree of life necklace and how the early Celts worshipped trees. They believed their ancestors lived in trees and are available to usher family members into eternity. Alex is fascinated by the Celts.

"You have to have a tree of life necklace. It's part of your heritage, babe."

"He's a good man," Gertrude says, removing the necklace from the case.

I didn't know it then, but I would start wearing the tree of life necklace every day after the governor declared a state of emergency in Denver a couple weeks after we returned from London. *COVID-19* would become as familiar as *hello* and *goodbye* in daily conversations.

"Would either of you like a tarot reading?" Gertrude asks. "I have Fionna here next week. She's one of my best readers."

Alex declines a reading, but Zoe is up for it. She's trying to understand why being in London has been difficult. She thinks it might be bad karma. We both set appointments with Fionna for early next week.

34

Ashes to Ashes

"Ashes to ashes, dust to dust," the priest says. The congregation of worshipers files into the cathedral to get their foreheads crossed with ashes, reminding them that life has an expiration date. Instead of getting in line, Zoe and I light candles below a statue of Saint Anthony, known as the saint who finds lost things. I feel a little lost today as the headlines in the London newspapers get worse each day. Should we get masks, rubber gloves, and antibacterial soap?

After the Ash Wednesday service, a parishioner approaches me. "You look like a character in *Fleabag*. Weren't you in season two, the one with the sexy priest?"

"It would be just like me to hook up with a sexy priest, sir, but no, I'm not Phoebe Waller-Bridge. There was a dynamic priest who flirted with me in the late eighties. Thanks for thinking I could be on TV, though."

Zoe tugs on my gray cashmere sweater, reminding me we have tarot readings in half an hour. She pays for five more votive candles for her flatmates. We bless ourselves before leaving, then grab a quick espresso from a street vendor on our way to Lotus Heart Bookstore.

Gertrude, a middle-aged woman with pinkish gold hair, greets Zoe for the first time. She offers each of us one long, white feather, which she claims will give us a good reading.

Fionna, the reader, takes Zoe first.

Gertrude looks surprisingly like my Aunt Gertrude on the Morrison side. I wish I had a photo of my aunt with me. Aunt Gertrude was born in the thirties and, as life-long single women, earned the title Eccentric Old Maid. She supported herself by buying vintage clothing from estate sales and reselling them from her Brooklyn apartment. Her boutique-like setting attracted women who came by appointment to purchase the clothing. Thanks to Aunt Gertrude's success, I inherited a small amount of money and some of the vintage clothing after she passed. Gertrude never had children of her own. I must have been five years old the one and only time I met her.

I remember September 10, 1962, the day a West Virginia lawyer delivered my inheritance check. It was a complete shock to me, a lawyer requesting to meet me in the lobby of my dorm! My first thought was I must have finally been caught buying alcohol with my older roommate's driver's license. *Oh shit, I really have to stop drinking so much rum and Coke.*

The lawyer, I think his last name was Prichard, greeted me with a check and a fuchsia suitcase full of flapper dresses, cloche hats, and lace collars that looked like pieces from *The Great Gatsby*. They might have made F. Scott Fitzgerald cry.

I remember the lawyer saying, "It's alright, miss, stop bowing, miss, you don't owe me anything. Maybe say a few prayers for the deceased, that's all. Good day."

When he left, I fell to my knees right there in the lobby. I even sang a few hymns I was pretty sure weren't Catholic, followed by, "Thank you, Jesus, and amen!"

Since I had very little spending money at WVU, I considered Gertrude to be my benefactor of good times. While I used most of her money to supplement my partial scholarship, I used twenty dollars a week to eat meals away from the dorm, where my New York accent didn't go over at the dinner table. I lost track of how many times I was teased about the way I said "cawfee."

Five dollars a week got put in a jar to buy alcohol now and then. West Virginia was a dry state then. I had to go underground and use my roommate's ID for alcohol.

Gertrude was one of the religious Morrison clan and would not have approved of some of her money going toward funding parties in my dorm room. I'm sure she would have loved a piece of vintage jewelry I bought in her honor.

Zoe gives me a quick hug before Fionna leads me downstairs. I plan to finish a conversation about tarot with Gertrude after my reading. The small room at the bottom of the stairs is dark and cold. The faded, sepia walls are missing any type of decoration; the environment is dull and unappealing.

Fionna, a thin, soft-spoken woman, starts our session by laying down a royal blue velvet cloth with an embossed silver moon in the center and gold stars around the edges. The cloth is the only attractive thing on the table. She instructs me to make three piles of cards.

"Choose one of the piles, then access your unconscious and take ten cards from that pile."

I do as she tells me and watch her arrange the ten cards in a particular order.

"Your life will radically change this year, Diane."

Won't everyone's, I think. Damn, I paid a lot of money for this reading.

So as to avoid judging Fionna, I stop looking at her or the cards for a moment and let myself go inward. I'm not aware of what Fionna is saying, although I do hear her say my company name. I can hear footsteps on the floor above and the sound of a bell as a new customer enters the store, but I know it's time to get back to the reading.

"Being more creative will help you start a new venture in the future. Whatever you choose to do will flourish due to your youthful spirit," Fionna claims.

"Do you know what the new venture might be, Fionna?"

"Please wait until the end of the reading to ask questions," she says, as if the spirits won't be happy if I change her rules.

The justice card surfaces, which Fionna says has something to do with signing documents, perhaps for publishing a book. The numbers seven and ten are significant in defining projects that are pending.

"The number seven is particularly significant for you, a lucky number, or seven aspects of yourself, perhaps?"

Well, seven is the number of my Enneagram personality type. I have had seven nicknames in my life. I know there are seven colors in the rainbow, seven is significant in most religions, and there are seven dwarfs in *Snow White*.

Getting back to the justice card and signing documents. Craig and I will be signing several contracts starting in March because we are forced to refinance our rental property on Maui. The island would not allow anyone to be there without agreeing to a fourteen-day quarantine. We obviously fall into deep debt because our property remains empty through 2020.

"You're cheeky in the eyes, Diane. You can charm a crowd in a flash, which is a trait that will continue to bring you wealth. You can be a Diva sometimes, and some people find the pretentious side of you charming.

Those who like your style will continue to follow you when you start a new company," Fionna continues.

"I'm outspoken, irreverent, and a bit of a stand-up comic who gets the most profound messages out in a light-hearted way. I do use what you Brits call *taboo* words to solicit a specific reaction from an audience. It seems to be my way of having a succinct expression of frustration when I curse, although I rarely say *fuck*."

Reflecting back on my meeting with Fionna, there are three things I note in my journal. I need to balance helping creative people with nurturing my own creativity. My memoir may be finished sooner than I expected. A new business venture is coming in the next couple of years.

Fionna, like Dora, mentions that Robert protects me. I never thought much about the fact that my father's heritage was half Brit and half Irish. I understand now why Robert fell in love with Veronica, an extrovert compared to most of his family, which tended to be reserved and judgmental. My mother was probably a breath of fresh air compared to them. No wonder Veronica protected me from the Morrisons. I thought it was pride on her part, but I see it differently now that I'm immersed in British culture here in London.

Fionna finishes our session with a sketch of a large, numinous being who appears to be a black angel without wings—maybe a prophet?

"Blessing and safe journey back to the States, Diane," Fionna says, as she hands me her signed sketch.

I attribute my sudden burst of energy the next morning to the fact a divine being, like in Fionna's sketch, appeared in my dream last night. Perhaps he will guide me through the troubled times ahead.

The day before Alex and I leave London, I return to my favorite cafe. The three of us had gone there several times during our visit, but today I'm alone.

The Gardenia Tea Store, just around the corner from the British Museum, is painted the color of pistachio ice cream. After I walk through the front door surrounded by white gardenia stencils, Abdul, the owner, greets me before he turns on the store's small red and white chandeliers. I'm the first one here this morning. I check all the small, white tables surrounded by chairs with bright lime cushions and choose the table in the back corner of the room. Abdul fixes my tea himself while his staff, three beautiful young girls, arrange the bright-colored tea tins on the carefully organized wooden shelves. He serves my tea in a light blue, iron pot. I sip it slowly from a small matching cup. The delicate structure of the tea enters me as my eyes close. I feel my body shimmer and swirl like the steam coming from my cup. After several minutes, my face feels numb. I enter a peaceful state of mind for twenty minutes as I slowly sip the tea.

After a while, Abdul senses he can approach me. Today he lays down two rose biscuits on a clear glass plate in front of me. When he asks how well one of his stores would do in California, I suggest San Francisco or West Hollywood. Abdul scrunches his face as if he's caught between the thrill of trying something new and resistance to the hard work it would take to make his dream of having a store in California come true. His previously mellow personality is starting to show excitement.

"You are going for it, aren't you Abdul? Will I see you in California sometime this year?" I ask.

He nods. "You know when you first sat down in the store, I thought you were a typical American woman, only interested in material things and

209

seeing London in a hurry. You are much more! I will pray my five daily prayers for you. Muslims pray Salat at dawn, midday, dusk, after sunset, and between sunset and midnight. We have always done ritualistic washings like world governments are requiring now. You must protect yourself, Diane. I'm afraid the virus is about to get out of control." He hands me a four-ounce bag of milky oolong tea to take home.

The door of the Gardenia Tea Store rattles as I walk outside. The cold air sends a chill down my spine. When I return to the hotel, I speak more softly because I have been meditating with tea. I'm grateful for Abdul's prayers as I begin to realize the world is never going to be quite the same again in my lifetime.

Fionna's reading makes more sense to me after I leave London. The flight home on British Airways is just a hint of what's to come. The flight, which is two-thirds empty, feels eerie. Most of the passengers are wearing black face masks and clear latex gloves. I feel as if we are all characters in a science fiction series on Netflix. I picture myself in a black mask and large black Prada sunglasses. Is that look going to be typical for me? At least I'll save money on makeup! What about my hair? Will any hairdresser take me for a cut and color? My red hair is down to my shoulders and starting to turn gray.

The stewardess delivers my meal and two small bottles of red wine, either because she wants me to fall asleep as soon as possible or as compensation for the fact that this plane is seemingly going to land on a planet far, far away. I plug in my earphones and take out the journal I bought at Heathrow Airport before we boarded. My fingers touch the gold embossed letters on the cover: *Make It Happen.*

35

Raw

There's not much difference between being in London and being in Denver in early March. Both places are raw. We get about three weeks of spring in Denver and it sure as hell doesn't start on March 21. When we land in Denver, the virus panic is in the air. Even our positive-thinking Uber driver tells us we have to wear masks, which he provides. There's not much conversation on the ride home because talking spreads the disease, we've been told. Tim usually keeps us entertained with stories about his next trip to a destination in a remote location.

"Traveling is going to become very difficult now," he says.

"Guess we won't be seeing you for a while, Tim. Stay safe!"

The moody darkness in London follows us to Denver, but this environment and the subtle signs of spring help me hold on to what's real. I see a crocus poking through a small patch of snow.

As soon as we disarm the alarm system, bring our luggage inside, and pull off our masks, life feels normal for a minute. The small card Fionna gave me sits on top of a tin of biscuits. It reads: *Forgiveness is giving up all hope of having had a different past. Stay healthy! Fionna.*

I wake up feeling jet lagged at 4 a.m. and reach for the white Le Creuset coffee pot sitting on a side table beside my bed. I pour myself a small cup of coffee before checking my text messages.

"Zoe's roommate, Issy, tested positive for the virus. Issy has been moved to a different flat. She and her boyfriend were probably infected on their trip to Milan during spring break. The two of them are lucky they made it back to London. There's a rumor the Italian borders are going to be closed within days."

"Oh my God, Craig, is Zoe going to be tested?"

"Testing isn't easy in London, or for that matter, here in California. We're expecting CU to send Zoe home in the next couple of weeks. Let's face it, our leaders didn't take a proactive approach against COVID-19 like other countries like China, Korea, and Germany did."

The yard, covered with snow, resembles the high contrast of a black-and-white photograph. The day is cold and stark. Schools and some businesses are closed. When I taught elementary school, I always loved a snow day. A snow day was a day to play games, bake cookies, and read with Michelle and Craig.

Today is going to be a pajama day for me. I wonder how many Divas secretly love pajama days like I do. I don't feel much like a Diva today though, slouched in the big, overstuffed yellow chair in the Blue Room. I remain positive, avoiding the worst case scenarios about Zoe's roommate testing positive.

Zoe may have to return to California by herself. I can be a moral support, FaceTiming her as often as she needs. Craig will have to cancel their flights to Paris, a trip supposed to be a glorious ending to Zoe's junior year in London. I can pay for the fees he might incur for flight changes. After I finish my list of possibilities to help my granddaughter, I realize Zoe will probably be supporting me instead of me supporting her. She is one of my idols, so strong and proactive at twenty-one—a real goal-setter.

Life becomes mechanical fast. We go through our first month in quarantine with an antiseptic attitude: washing our hands for twenty seconds, changing towels daily, keeping our hands away from our faces, having groceries delivered, wearing masks when we leave the house, cleaning the whole house twice a week, cooking all of our meals at home.

I'm becoming like Marion Cunningham, the perfect wife in *Happy Days*. Are we going back in time? Are we living in the seventies?

The salons are all closed. I go through my closets searching for hats, scarves, and an old wig to cover up the gray hair coming in. My witchy fingernails look like dried-up yellow daggers, since Amazon is restricting non-essential purchases such as nail clippers and emery boards. At least I have a year's supply of polish from Bon Marché in Paris.

Diva's aren't made, they're born! I came into this world with a million-to-one chance of survival, and I'm sure as hell not going to lose my cheeky attitude now. Just keep your shit together with style, I tell myself every day.

Diva is my mask. Smart is my super power. I can't hide from who I am because I will burn up inside. I feel like I'm right back where I was when I was diagnosed with breast cancer. Just do the next right thing, I tell myself. What else can I do in the middle of a pandemic?

I lick the salt on my margarita as I look through an old journal I used when I was part of a writing group (really more of a therapy group with plenty of crying going on). This dribble doesn't motivate me to write tonight. I better get online to order a six-month supply of the things on our list of essentials.

It's becoming hard to get toilet paper, antiseptic soap, Purell, Clorox wipes, etc. Some people are buying large amounts of the items we desperately need and reselling them at inflated prices. I see one roll of toilet paper for twenty-five dollars on eBay. We have a month's supply of toilet paper, if we monitor how much we use. Toilet paper is for poop; facial tissues are for pee.

An artist friend of ours does an oil painting of a single roll of toilet paper titled *Give Them What They Want*. When she makes prints of the piece, she can hardly keep up with the demand.

No matter how much I practice mindfulness, stay positive, and pray for the pandemic to be contained, I sense the earth is being torn apart. Is this what Saint John of the Cross meant by the dark night of the soul, *noche oscura del alma*? The only light in this dark night is the light that comes from the soul.

Thank God, Zoe made it home safe. That girl is a trooper, still smiling after a gruesome twelve-hour flight from London and a three-hour wait to be tested at LAX. She's exhausted, but clear of the virus. Alex and I celebrate Zoe's return to California with a bottle of Laurent-Perrier Champagne at 6 a.m. When in doubt, pretend you're French. Profite de la vie!

Knowing we won't get out of survival mode soon, I'm concerned Alex's explosive anger, an extension of his normal anxiety, will surface. I need to get away from him, but where the hell can I go? I'm a victim of the stay-at-home order in Denver. Since we're sleeping in separate rooms, I lock the Blue Room door when Alex's temper escalates.

It's two days before the Fourth of July weekend. I get up early, put out the ingredients for breakfast, and set the table in the small sitting room. Thank God I bought a turntable and speakers a month before we left the country. I fill my soul with pop music: Harry Styles, Billie Eilish, and Taylor Swift. Breakfast is when Alex and I connect. It could be the source of light and the courtyard view of our front French garden that calms him. By the time Alex sits down, I'm singing "Ocean Eyes" along with Billie Eilish.

The conversation today is about how to expand our herb garden and buying new lingerie. We have seedlings growing in small glass candleholders on a window sill. The thought of having greens growing inside the house makes us happy. Alex had to use last year's seeds; new seeds are back ordered for months. Our grandson Jeremy, who raises chickens, offers to help us set up a coop in our backyard. It feels good to be more self-sustaining.

"Babe, you need more lingerie. You don't wear real clothes inside the house. Why don't you order a couple of strappy nightgowns from the store in Charleston?"

"I have a silver one and a black one."

"Get a red one!" he says with a nasty grin.

We watch movies to take our minds off the news, ones that take us to France like *Midnight in Paris*, or that take us into the past, like *The Great Gatsby*. Sometimes I dress like one of the characters. It's easy for me to be Carey Mulligan as Daisy in *The Great Gatsby*; I have plenty of flapper dresses from Aunt Gertrude and jewelry from Tiffany's Jazz Age collection.

TV shows are dwindling fast. *American Idol* does a good job with Zooming contestant performances. Katy Perry, one of the judges, dresses as an antiviral soap dispenser in the first episode of the show during lockdown.

I have too much idle time because my speaking engagements are canceled for the rest of the year. Conference rooms will probably become sleeping rooms before long. My online company of classes keeps us afloat for now.

Living a life in quarantine had been normal since childhood, since my mother kept me in the house all the time. In a way, I'm better prepared to deal with COVID-19 than most people. I'm temporarily caught in a memory from 1951.

I was nine when Veronica insisted on keeping me home from school for three weeks. I wasn't sick, and I had already missed forty days of third grade that year.

My uncle Skip stopped by for breakfast one morning. Veronica was hung over on the living room couch. If she had been awake, she would have screamed at Addie for letting Skip in the kitchen. Since Skip wasn't allowed in my room, he helped me with my math problems from outside my bedroom door.

"Veronica says I'm filthy, Cookie, but listen, I take a shower at the YMCA every night. I'm probably cleaner than her."

"You look handsome, Skip. Your clothes are nicer than what Pop wears when he's relaxing around the house."

When Addie left the kitchen, Skip handed me a note with the word *Munchausen's* on it.

"Give this to your teacher. Your mother has a disease. You're not a sickly girl, Cookie. Veronica needs you to keep her company at home. You need to be in school!" Skip opens my bedroom window before he leaves. I love the smell of fresh air. Then Veronica comes into the room.

"You'll catch your death, Cookie. I hear a wheeze in your lungs. Addie might have to put a plaster on your back tonight. You don't want to have pneumonia again, do you?"

"I'm going to school tomorrow. You can't stop me!" I screamed. "Sam says you need to stop keeping me home from school. It's against the law."

I watched Veronica go back into the kitchen, wearing a mask after she found out Skip was there. She used disinfectant and candles to get rid of what she called "Skip's stink." When Addie mentioned Skip had helped me with homework, Veronica gave her a nasty look.

Since I can't leave my house to visit Dora during the pandemic, I give her a call because the current quarantine is bringing up my restricted life as a child.

"Being pretentious allowed you to wear masks as a child, Diane. Perhaps like any good performer, you lived in a fantasy world when you were a child. Your family was beyond dysfunctional. Fortunately there was always one person who acted normal on any particular day. Yes, it is true that your mother had a mild case of Munchausen's Disease."

"Am I still pretentious at seventy-seven, Dora?"

"You'll always be a pretentious Diva. If you lived in Japan, you would be called a *wise woman*, a term used for people between sixty and eighty. Many Japanese people live past a hundred. You can't stop growing now. You're a new bud ready to blossom again. Never stop being a Diva."

I answer Dora with one of my favorite quotes by Anais Nin, saying, "And the risk to remain tight in a bud was more than the risk to blossom."

Chances are no one will notice me writing on my front porch today, but I still freshen my bright red lipstick, straighten my turquoise Tiffany ring, and put on my black Prada sunglasses.

"You're a true creative, writing in the midst of this chaos," my neighbor says, peering over the gate.

I eventually end the conversation the way I end every conversation these days. "Stay healthy!"

Scott calls while I'm writing.

"I read your latest entry. I want you to crawl inside the reader's head when you write from now on. Ground your writing in space and time. When you're writing a memory, let the reader know. It's like you're pausing a movie. Put memories in italics and write those lines in past tense. Try these ideas. We'll talk again next week. You got this!"

Upside Down March 2020

Diane Morrison

Fish fell out of water

Bird stuck on the ground

Chaos giving orders

Everything upside down

A kettle gleams on the stove when I go back inside to make tea. It's not a particularly expensive kettle, but its elegant design makes it stand out. I fill the kettle, take time to watch the steam come out of the spout as it heats, and put a towel over my head to breathe in the steam like I did when I was a kid.

The kettle stops whistling after I pour the water into my small teapot from the Gardenia Tea Store. After I meditate over the milky oolong tea, I promise myself I will take the high road in difficult situations from now on. The pandemic isn't going to last forever. I want to come out of it with more compassion.

My friend Bruce left a small card on the porch the previous evening. There are three pressed pansies inside with a note: *Nothing lasts forever!*

Bruce loves pansies, though they don't last through the summer. Is he telling me my former life will return someday?

36

Full Circle

Zoe is safe! I'm able to reflect back on what I learned about her during our stay in London. In spite of the virus, I knew I may never have twelve days of quality time with my granddaughter again.

She's twenty-one and finishing her degree in communications. I want to be like Zoe. She's someone who loves the earth and all beings. She's an activist who's well-versed in women's rights, climate change, and the importance of a vegan diet.

Her lifestyle inspires me to consider changes in my own life. First I need to strip down to the bare essentials of who I am. In other words, I have to be willing to get below my masks and dig deeper to find what Carl Jung calls the *Self*. Basically, the plan is to make my unconscious conscious, a frightening undertaking during such a perilous time.

Should I watch a thriller tonight instead to give myself an even bigger scare before I turn in for the night? Instead, I go to my old basement, built in 1900, to talk to my unconscious, or God, I suppose. I brush away a spider's nest, find a small wooden bench, and use my vipassana meditation to help me go deep.

I remember guru Steve's words, "Just let your thoughts pass through. Don't try to stop them. Focus on your breath." Three hours later, I surface from what I call sacred space. It's 2 a.m., I can hear Alex snoring. I must admit, I sleep like a baby, but I don't encounter God. It wasn't as powerful as the night Scott said that I became love.

I recall something else Carl Jung once said: "People will do anything, no matter how absurd, in order to avoid their own souls. One does not become enlightened by imagining figures of light, but by making darkness conscious."

Am I avoiding my soul because I can't give up my image? Maybe all my nicknames need to go away. Rare Orchid, Tough Cookie, Ginger, Princess, Gypsy, Diva, and Collector. Then there's my name, Diane, because my mother wanted me to be a goddess. Damn, I could stand to get rid of some of those labels. Well, maybe I'll keep Diva for a little longer.

"Wait now, Dr. Jung, can you hear me in the spirit realm? Listen, I can't give up all of my addictions. Some aren't too bad. I've never been an alcoholic."

"Who are you talking to, babe? It's the middle of the night. Go to bed. You need your sleep. Take a melatonin. It's on the list of things to fight COVID-19."

Thank God the governor has changed the stay-at-home order to safer-at-home. Alex was right: being stuck in the house for so long has made me a little weird. Today is the day I get to turn the brass handle on the front door to go outside beyond the gate. Oh wow! I feel as if I just got out of prison. People walking by look at me as if I'm a messenger of death because I'm an older woman. I know what minorities feel like more than ever now. I feel like I am a minority for the first time in my life because I am in the age group most at risk. Even my friends and family look at me differently because I am always wearing a mask. Strangers look scared of me.

I walk on side streets at first because anyone over the age of sixty out walking is fair game for criticism. Many young people and politicians have made it clear: older Americans should give up their lives to save the young. I'm faced with my own lack of courage about who I am as an aging woman. Since I have an overly positive attitude about life, I never think of myself as anyone other than an adolescent in an adult body. My own mortality had always stayed in the background until I had breast cancer. I'm not afraid to die, I just don't think about it much. Courage is the ability to do something out of my comfort zone. Do I have to think about funeral arrangements? Damn, I can't do that!

Fortunately, Kara, my grandson's wife, made me ten new colorful masks she described as "edgy, perfect for a Diva." Small surprises do so much for the soul. These masks are more important to me than my designer clothes. Plus, getting anything in the mail is a big deal in confinement. When I add a cool pair of sunglasses to my look, I feel confident and ready to be kind to the youngsters who get a kick out of making fun of me.

"Have a nice day, stay safe now. Try a mask!" I say with conviction. Eventually, I begin to get compliments. I even get interesting responses from some of the former intimidators, like "You look good, miss!" or "I like your mask."

If I can continue to build my courage, will I spend my later years marching for political causes like Zoe. Or will I get the word out about our changing world through my writing?

Thinking of writing, I can't afford to work with Scott anymore, which is unfortunate. We have a strong chemical connection, not unlike Pablo Picasso and Dora Maar, or Édouard Manet and Berthe Morisot. Scott posts a video of his dog Fitz, short for Fitzgerald, running free in Boulder Canyon. I can see Fitz, but I can't see Scott. I can hear the sound of Scott's breathing. I wonder if I will ever really be free of this rugged, earthy, brilliant writer who came into my life to torture me with his selflessness and sensuality. I sip my oolong tea from the Gardenia Tea Store and listen to Scott's breathing one more time.

When I get around to reading *The New York Times* this morning, it's clear people are dying fast, especially in New York. My cousin talks about ice trucks carrying bodies to cemeteries. Only family members can oversee a simple burial. There's no opportunity for eulogies or normal closure with loved ones, since such gatherings would exacerbate the virus's spread. Sadly, these loved ones may not get over this for a long time. Many of them are already reporting symptoms of post-traumatic stress.

One of the positive things about the virus is that people are praying again.

I remember spying on Addie saying her black Rosary with a silver cross and tiny medals when I was a little girl. "Hail Mary, full of grace. The Lord is with thee." I take out Addie's old Rosary, which she gave me before she died, attempting to pray myself to sleep.

Many friends close to my age are making funeral arrangements, but what would a funeral look like now? The only people who are continuing to maintain their burial traditions are the Hasidic Jews. They honor their dead with lengthy ceremonies and celebrations as they always have. Sadly, many of them have tested positive after these gatherings.

According to the media, time is stacked against me. I can't escape thinking about my mortality. Is Heaven real? Is an afterlife only available after many lifetimes or spending time in Bardo or Purgatory? Turn the clock ahead to when things are better, please!

There's a rebellion brewing inside me. The rebellious teen from the fifties is still in me. Like the sixteen-year-old at the Academy, red is still my signature color: red hair, red nails, and bright red lipstick. I wear something red every day during lockdown. Roses are red, red means good luck in Asian cultures, and red captures attention. I need attention because I don't like feeling old. I agree with Howard Stern, who claims he never intends to grow up.

My hairdresser, Riley, keeps me young by reminding me I'm a Diva. He says, "There are two types of Divas in the world: Divas and everyone else."

I arrive at the salon, check the time on my dashboard, and call Riley before I leave the car. When I enter the salon, my nose starts dripping. I remove my mask, wipe my nose, Purell my hands, and start the whole protected process of getting a haircut again. I feel naked when my makeup-less face is exposed for a few seconds as I remove my mask to deal with the runny nose. Riley notices my freckles. He has never seen me without makeup. I'm pretty sure he's lying when he tells me I look cute.

When I realize I don't care if I wear makeup anymore, I know I'm starting to see through my Diva-ness. Self isn't getting underneath the Diva, it's hard-wired into me. Finding Self is about accepting all parts of myself—pretentious and real. It's all good!

"My life has been a wild journey, Riley. You know how it all began in Jersey City decades ago, how childhood drama made me a Diva who used performance to survive an alcoholic environment, and how a rigid, cold marriage almost destroyed me. It continued into midlife after my divorce when I became a successful Diva, living the good life in spite of the painful past."

"It really is about time, Diane. Maybe our lives seem frozen right now, but we need to have the courage to move on."

Alex loves my short, purple hair. I'm no longer a redhead.

A perfect harvest moon brings us into the French garden tonight. My lips quiver when I speak to my husband about love. "Is love actually a magnetic pull between souls? Is it not a person we fall in love with so much as a love for a portrait of that person we create? I'm attracted to you, Alex, because you're an artist, a man who lives outside the box."

"I agree. I love you too, babe."

Thinking back to why I divorced Anthony, when I contrast my marriage with Alex, our personalities do bridge. An observer feeds me with wisdom and never tries to tame my wildness. We do help each other grow and flourish. I'm not good at easy things, like booking flights or doing FaceTime. Alex helps me with those things. He's not good at planning things like reading memos or following recipes. I help him set goals and go over the last memo he's burned.

"Alex, did you see the memo I put on your desk a few minutes ago?"

"Tomorrow is another day! By the way, do you think Jesus wrote in the sand? I like his style of goal-setting, but I guess we don't have any sand," he laughs.

Alex insists on getting me one more nightcap, a rich combination of salted caramel liquor, tequila, and mezcal. We sit together, looking at a Hicks painting of two lovers. It's in the painter's new style, a departure from his early paintings, with more of a Rembrandt aesthetic. No matter what Hicks paints, he never considers the work to be complete until his mind, body, and soul can release it.

The windows are open in the sitting room the next morning. Alex and I begin our day with gluten-free blueberry muffins and cold brew coffee with oat milk. We have an interview with the editor of *Fine Art Connoisseur* magazine this afternoon. We're one of four collectors featured in the annual issue. In a sense, the article honors us as top collectors in the US.

When I was young, I couldn't afford to buy paintings, so I used my imagination. I collected rocks, sea shells, and rough-edged pieces of beach glass. I filled frames with my sketches and watercolor paintings. Beauty gave me a type of protection as a child. When things were difficult, I escaped into a world of beauty. I also collected journals, spiral notebooks, and pieces of wrapping paper for writing. I created an entire journal on my collection of Madame Alexander dolls.

Creativity has always been my truest world.

Before the magazine interview, I need to spend time with a painting I started last week. It was a wild night of drinking wine and throwing Prussian blue and canary yellow paint on a Jackson-Pollock-style abstract piece. I'd felt like Pollock, totally losing track of space and time as I painted the canvas on the floor.

There are house-painting brushes, squirt guns, tooth brushes, even turkey basters left next to the canvas. I'm only interested in painting from the unconscious now. I can still hear my mentor, Charles, telling me, "Never let your audience know you hesitate when you paint."

While I finish up in the studio, Alex goes into his office to read the questions from the editor for the magazine. He creates a file of his answers. Meanwhile, rather than answering every question, I create a narrative about my life as an art collector:

I started sketching and painting when I was ten, inspired by my mother's design sense, an uncle who designed hotels, and an aunt who designed lingerie.

In 1981, while healing from breast cancer, I used pastels on paper to convey images that came to me while I meditated.

I later earned a master's degree in art and psychology, with a thesis focused on art as healing. During that time, I also had a show of my paintings and writings at the University of Colorado.

My husband, Alex, and I have been collecting oil paintings from galleries in Denver, Los Angeles, New York, San Francisco, and Paris for almost twenty years. We believe having a connection with the artists we collect is important.

In 2014, we visited the best venue for contemporary realism in Paris. We immediately fell in love with its owners, Yann and Laetitia. We returned to the gallery in 2015 for Nicholas Martin's one-man show, after we saw his work at the gallery in Paris the prior year.

In 2016, we invited Martin to stay with us in Denver. The French painter made quite an impression in Denver and now shows regularly at Abend Gallery. We call the art we collect now: realistic art with an edge.

In closing, I suggest taking the risk to be brave enough to live artfully. You have to leave your comfort zone and go into your intuition. You can't get there on a jet, only by risk. What you discover there will be beautiful. What you discover will be yourself.

37

Ageless

It's 6 a.m., and I'm standing on the edge of the front courtyard, listening to early morning birds and looking at the sparkling dewdrops on the redbud tree. The violet blossoms are long gone, but bright green, heart-shaped leaves remain.

When I was a little girl, I liked to pretend dewdrops were evidence of a fairy visiting. It was as if Tinkerbell had dropped by to say hello. Tinkerbell and Peter Pan were my favorite characters in literature. Peter, obsessed with his shadow, reminds me of myself. My shadow is psychological and one that I've long-tried to suppress.

Just for fun, I walk on the front sidewalk to catch a look at my physical shadow as the sun comes up. I see a dark carbon copy of myself. Didn't Peter Pan say he couldn't leave his shadow lying around and not miss it sooner or later?

The book was written by J. M. Barrie. When the author's brother died at fourteen, their mother referred to her dead son as a "forever boy." It was Disney Studios who made Peter Pan a famous character—a charming boy who never wanted to grow up, or more likely didn't want to die. Peter Pan is a perfect example of Carl Jung's child archetype—one who struggles with leaving the paradise of childhood. The famous psychiatrist would call Peter Pan a classic *puer*.

Damn, is that you, C. J.? Are you here to tell me I really will never grow up? What is it you call me, a *puella*? I smell your pipe, and no one is around. Am I just being affected by last night's combination of melatonin and cannabis? It doesn't matter. Damn, am I just talking to myself again?

Before I continue to make a fool of myself, pretending to talk to a dead psychiatrist, I unravel a quote by Jung which I have posted in my writing closet: "One does not become enlightened by imagining figures of light, but by making the darkness conscious."

Who said I wanted to become enlightened? I'm okay with chasing my shadow. For God's sake, the Corona makes it easy to face one's shadow or inner dragons during quarantine. I have cabin fever of the worst kind. Even the most positive personality types have trouble saying something like "have a nice day" when it would be more honest to prepare them for a shitty day!

What I need is a tall cold brew coffee to clear my mind. I want to get to the bottom of what C. J. would tell me if he could speak.

"You are a classic *puella*, Diane. You can't admit you're aging. You had an overprotective mother, you expect men to serve you, you spend too much money, and you party too much!"

Damn it, I have to get out of here. I'm hallucinating. There's a drive-thru Starbucks about two miles away. I haven't driven my Audi since I bought it six months ago.

I drive past the park, catching the early runners and two or three people walking their dogs. I take a right onto a street that has an assortment of small houses, some of them kind of funky. My favorite is a bungalow decorated with a combination of Christmas lights, a blow-up jack-o'-lantern, and plastic flamingos spread out amongst a flower garden of bright zinnias. I can't help driving around the corner to see if any other holidays are represented in the backyard.

There are three pop-up tents, picnic tables, and barbecue grills back there. My God, have the owners taken in street people? Shelters aren't doing a good job of providing enough social distancing for those who no longer have homes. I imagine there will soon be more of these tents all over Denver.

Today I slipped some cash under the front door of the house. Tomorrow I will do a food order for the people living here.

I need to get out of the house more often. My mind is clear. I don't want to think about my good side or my dark side or the fact I'm a *puella* right now.

I finish my coffee and continue past more bungalows, boarded-up restaurants, a dog grooming place, and an assisted living facility. I take a left onto Bruce's street to remember all the good times we had sitting on his front porch. I have to pull over for a minute because I can't stop crying. I miss my friend so much. Bruce never wears a mask, though, so when he gestures through his kitchen window for me to come in, I wave and continue on.

The International Cannabis Church around the corner catches my eye after I leave Bruce's house. It's closed, like every church in Denver. It's amazing weed is one of the things several of my friends have offered me rather than the typical "I'm thinking of you" apple pie. I laugh hard when I think about how people see me.

I am heading home when I get a text from Alex. He wants to buy a Beatles album because "Sgt. Pepper's Lonely Hearts Club Band," his favorite, is one of the cuts. "Oh, and Carl Jung is on the front cover, babe."

"Sure, why not, the album cover sounds great!" I text back.

Jesus, what are the chances? C. J. and the Beatles?

Alex texts again. "I also got BTS's 2019 album *Map of the Soul*, which specifically focuses on Carl Jung's shadow and ego theories."

I can't seem to escape C. J. today. I find it interesting that I'm wearing a mask, when I want so much to get rid of my own masks. I get it: it's okay to protect my persona with a mask, but it's not okay to project my shadow on other people. Yes, I promise I will look at my own crap.

There it is, my arrogant side. I love being arrogant instead of dealing with my fearfulness. Yet, I know my questioning side has saved my life many times.

The thing is, I want to live out loud and continue to do risky things! I see where I've been and where I'm going. Unfortunately, my consulting company is ending, at least the teaching aspect of it. School districts are freezing teacher salaries due to lack of funding. It's time to create a new blueprint for my life. What is my next destination? I see myself doing motivational speaking, but not teaching anymore. This, I suppose, is my come-to-Jesus moment. What do I do now, at seventy-seven years old?

I reflect on my last face-to-face session with Dora when she said, "You're like a cat, Diane. You have strong bursts of energy, you land on your feet no matter what comes in your path, you can jump from one project to another, you squeeze your way out of tight situations, and you know how to escape trouble."

Dora had also reminded me to do something for myself every day during the pandemic. "Do for yourself what you would do for someone you love. We all need self-care besides washing our hands twenty-five times a day."

The sun is streaming into the Blue Room. I have overslept for the first time in five months. Alex is scrambling eggs and making toast. I put the kettle on for tea, set the table, and choose his favorite record by Bastille, a British alternative rock group named after Bastille Day. This morning's album is appropriately called *Doom Days*.

We tried to get tickets to see Bastille while in London in February. I was ardently looking forward to seeing the Palladium Theater in Soho. Listening to *Dooms Days* gives me an opportunity to discuss the pandemic with Alex.

"Alex, what are your thoughts on the pandemic? Not only is COVID-19 spreading all over our country, but it's also a global issue. How do you think the effects can be minimized? In the beginning, populations of people sixty and older were the most vulnerable. Now young people are propagating the virus!"

His eyes stay fixed on the garden outside the sitting room. I watch him go outside to pick a handful of orange zinnias for the breakfast table. When he returns, he says, "I pay attention to nature. It's a sequence of events. Nature is predictable. COVID-19 isn't predictable. It's impossible to sort through what politicians and medical experts are saying."

My own irascible habits cause my mind to go astray while he speaks, but I will walk around outside today to figure out if, in fact, nature is that predictable.

"Why don't we do something special today, babe?"

"What made you ask that? I had the same idea when I woke up this morning."

Before we make definite plans, we take our teacups outside to enjoy walking around, sipping tea in a light rain shower. We are like two little kids giggling in the rain.

A beautiful tabby cat with blue eyes walks across our fence.

"How many lives have you had so far, cat? You might be able to survive seven close calls. There's an old rumor heard in Spain: you have at least seven lives, some cultures even say nine," I say.

Is the Hindu goddess Shiva inviting me to go through a birth and rebirth experience this year? It could also be I'm stuck in the amygdala part of my brain and am not able to see where my life is going next.

Alex keeps his word about having a special day. After we came in from the rain, he massaged me with a body oil called Artemisia. The topper on the container is a small sculpture of Artemis, goddess of the hunt.

After morning sex, we cuddle for a long time. He tells me he feels as if nothing can hurt him when he cuddles. What is it with these observer types, like Alex, who research everything? He also mentions cuddling pumps up the immune system.

Night falls like a curtain that night, as do my thoughts. I'm going back to when I was six years old, singing Shirley Temple songs for my family. Maybe I was actually a character more than a performer. I do know, without a doubt, that I was a Diva.

I reflect on my visit to London, particularly on the effect I had on the staff at the hotel. I made them laugh. The concierge called me the Diva and the Queen.

I walk down to our original basement, which would make a great wine cellar. There it is, a dusty tin containing photographs of me from birth to six years old. Every photograph is dated and labeled with one of my nicknames, most often Diva.

Instead of hanging out in the past, I call a couple of spas, but they are all closed. I resort to a long soak in the clawfoot tub, put on comfortable clothes, and just chill. I resist the urge to listen to anything except the sound of the wind this late afternoon. I don't utter a sound. I receive this experience without analyzing it. My monkey mind is turned off. Later this afternoon, I will take in a cornflower blue sky.

"Shield me, sister sky. Like a diamond, I have many facets. I'm tired of not being my authentic self." After I speak these words, I regret having said them. It takes so much energy to change. I hate it when I sense I'm going soft. Wasn't it Philip Roth who said something like "we miss ourselves sometimes when we look for ourselves?"

I take a picture of the sky and wait an hour before I speak.

"Stand up, oh mighty Diva. Be free!" I shout.

"Are you talking to C. J. again, babe?"

"Nope, just myself. I'm done with Dr. Jung. I recently read he went a little bonkers at the end of his life."

I thought Alex would say I was going bonkers, too, but he didn't.

Now what? I've been teaching about personality types for twenty-one years. I know a little about my essence, my original face, and my Type 7 personality. I know I've been this type since age eleven, when Veronica married Sam and we left Jersey City. I have always kept a positive attitude. I understand now this may have been due in part to the fact that I always felt responsible for keeping my mother happy.

Dora told me a long time ago, "You are not your Enneagram type, your Myers-Briggs profile, or your astrology sign. You are never fixed—your authentic self is more of a sage than an adventurer now."

There's a sweetness in the air this Sunday morning in August. I stay in bed, soaking in the sunlight, letting my thoughts pass through like the beginning of meditation. I fold back the European duvet and go outside to check the morning sky. It's gray and violet with a faint outline of clouds.

Looks like another high-pollution day, dangerous for sensitive people. Brunch on the blue and white French table won't happen this morning, but I look forward to a well-constructed cocktail at happy hour tonight. Nothing gives me more emotional support than a perfect Cosmopolitan or a dirty vodka martini.

The air quality improves as the sun goes down. Alex and I won't be going inside tonight until the crickets stop chirping. I wonder what the moon will look like. It was blood red last night because of the poor air quality.

The next morning, Alex and I put on our newest masks from England, walk to the park, and sit on the steps of the boathouse.

"It's so unusual to see so many crows flying over the lake this early in the morning," Alex says.

"How many times have we used the word *unusual* lately, Alex? Maybe what we think is unusual is going to be usual in the future."

As I sit on the steps sipping my espresso, I begin to construct a plan to have an art event here at the boathouse next spring. I will include artists, gallery owners, and collectors on our guest list.

In the meantime, I will make a podcast for creatives, those like myself who live outside the box. We already have our blog in place. I will add writing in a couple of art magazines to my list of goals to complete before the event.

"What are you thinking about, babe?"

"A party next spring. I have plans. Talk at happy hour?"

Epilogue

When a creative lands on earth and their family isn't very creative, no one gets you. It's really not anyone's fault. Then, having a creative spirit makes you feel like an outsider, which in my case is a gift, because I see the world in a different way. Different things that happened to me were hard, but those things shook me out of my trance.

Acknowledgments

I celebrate all of you who taught me or encouraged me to write.

Sister George Carol: God bless you for giving me my first writing award in tenth grade and for never giving me demerits for my behavior.

Brad: Thank you for being my profoundly gifted coach and editor. I should change my will because I owe you so much, dear friend.

Alex: I am grateful that you are as obsessed with beauty as I am. I love you.

Kathy: Merci, madame, for making good suggestions about my writing.

Greg: A shout-out to you for being the first to proofread my debut book.

Shay: You know everything about me. Thank you for offering clues about how to make the memoir authentic.

Craig and Kristen: You are the best offspring ever born.

Jeremy, Kailey, Tasha, Zoe, and Ryan: I want to be more like all of you.

Blake and Sienna: I cannot wait to watch you grow up.

The Burke men: Thank you, brothers, for coming into my life in my teens.

Cousin Susan: You gave me childhood memories that will never be lost. Many thanks.

Aunt Irene: Hats off to the greatest Diva I have ever known. I miss you every day.

I bow to all who have taken this writing journey with me. Namaste.

—Diane

CPSIA information can be obtained
at www.ICGtesting.com
Printed in the USA
LVHW111353030321
680478LV00025B/507

9 781087 943480